FROM
Outreach
TO
Equity

Innovative Models
of Library Policy
and Practice

**OFFICE FOR LITERACY
AND OUTREACH SERVICES**

Edited by Robin Osborne

Foreword by Carla D. Hayden

American Library Association
Chicago   2004

MASTICS-MORICHES-SHIRLEY
COMMUNITY LIBRARY

Composition and design by ALA Editions in Berkeley and Sans Extended, using QuarkXPress 5.0 on a PC platform

Printed on 50-pound white offset, a pH-neutral stock, and bound in 10-point coated cover stock by Data Reproductions

The paper used in this publication meets the minimum requirements of American National Standard for Information Sciences—Permanence of Paper for Printed Library Materials, ANSI Z39.48-1992.♾

Library of Congress Cataloging-in-Publication Data

From outreach to equity : innovative models of library policy and practice / Office for Literacy and Outreach Services ; edited by Robin Osborne.
    p. cm.
Includes bibliographical references and index.
ISBN 0-8389-3541-9 (alk. paper)
   1. Library outreach programs—United States. 2. Libraries and community—United States. 3. Libraries and minorities—United States. I. Osborne, Robin, 1954-
II. American Library Association. Office for Literacy and Outreach Services.
Z711.7.F76 2004
021.2—dc22   2004004480

Printed in the United States of America

08   07   06   5   4   3   2

CONTENTS

Models

Part 4
Technical Services: Connecting Minds   *66*
Zora J. Sampson

Models

FOREWORD

Carla D. Hayden
Executive Director, Enoch Pratt Free Library
ALA President, 2003–4

WELCOME TO *FROM OUTREACH TO EQUITY: INNOVATIVE MODELS OF LIBRARY POLICY and Practice,* which addresses a fundamental value of all library services and one of the key action areas of the American Library Association (ALA). This publication provides a contemporary view of library outreach for today's library managers, administrators, advocates, and staff. Its intent is to strengthen the focus of the profession while providing access to outreach-in-action models.

I am proud to support this book as part of my ALA presidential initiative during 2003–4. Herein you will hear fresh voices documenting exciting programs and their impact on local communities. Although most programs in this book are targeted to special populations, the overall goal for any library is to include these groups in its overall mission and strategies. Libraries also need clearly stated and creative action plans that will ensure successful outcomes. The commitment to inclusive service delivery means involvement of the entire community and all community stakeholders.

This book also celebrates the work of ALA's Office for Literacy and Outreach Services and other association units that support libraries in their efforts to serve traditionally underserved populations. The articles here highlight the diversity of local library initiatives in our communities and the wealth of resources available through ALA. Hopefully, readers will also explore ALA's website (www.ala.org) for additional resources that can help us meet the goals of inclusive service delivery.

I extend heartfelt appreciation to editor Robin Osborne, the six primary content contributors, and the forty-plus library practitioners who have described the results of their efforts. Thanks also to the association staffs who not only helped with this book but who also sustained ALA for the benefit of continued development and professional growth of the membership. So read, learn, and connect to make sure that there is truly Something for Everyone@ Your Library!

INTRODUCTION

Satia Marshall Orange
Office for Literacy and Outreach Services
American Library Association
Chicago, Illinois

Robin Osborne
Westchester Library System
Ardsley, New York

LIBRARIES AS WE KNOW THEM HAVE EVOLVED THROUGH THE CENTURIES FROM WELL-preserved private collections for royalty and the wealthy to the free and open environments many people enjoy today in the United States. The Library Bill of Rights published by the American Library Association (ALA) "affirms that all libraries are forums for information and ideas, and that . . . books and other library resources should be provided for the interest, information, and enlightenment of all people of the community the library serves."[1]

However, we need to understand that we have yet to achieve our goal of providing access to information for all that want and need it.

Historically, our solution to addressing the information needs of the "under" or "unserved" populations is through library outreach services. We can identify many examples of services provided to underserved groups. These outreach services often take place off site; are often dependent on special funding; are often administered by special staff. It is time for new ideas and language to help us reach our goal.

In the summer of 2003, ALA President Carla D. Hayden wrote:

> At a time when our public is challenged on multiple fronts, we need to recommit ourselves to the ideal of providing equal access to everyone, anywhere, anytime, and in any format. . . . By finally embracing equity of access we will be affirming our core values, recognizing realities, and assuring our future.[2]

In writing this book, we identified the need to shift focus from developing special services for specific user groups with funds that may disappear at any time to sustaining quality services for all user groups at all times. If we reframe what we know as *outreach* so that it is based upon "equity" rather than underserved populations, we can open a new window to information access and, more importantly, service delivery. Equity of access implies an ideal of fairness and balance and thus an appraisal of all components of the landscape in which we operate. To realize this ideal, we must reach inside to assess whether our internal policies, practices, and behaviors do or do not provide services to the totality of our communities. In other words, equity of access cannot be achieved without *equitable service delivery*.

Equitable service delivery must be the standard for all library services. To that end, we must ask ourselves:

> Do we recognize the diversity of our staff and our service populations, and do we value their input and perspective as we develop strategic plans?

> Do we evaluate all of our collections with fair and balanced criteria (e.g., should we use the same criteria to evaluate a literacy collection and a fiction collection)?

> Do we collaborate with colleagues as well as with members of the communities we serve to make sure our services are qualitative and effective (e.g., do we ask diverse representatives of our users to review and critique the content and structure of our Web pages)?

In this book we have highlighted model policies and practices that reflect equitable service delivery in a variety of library organizations rather than the multiple "other" special populations who may be included in a community's service delivery area. This book is for library staff, administrators, and trustees to use for assessment and planning. We hope the articles will help you focus on systemic strategies for library services that are inclusive, long-term, and based on the principles of fairness and balance.

LIMITATIONS OF OUTREACH AS POLICY MODEL

The concept of outreach evolved from the understanding that libraries do not attract and serve everyone. The term is often used to describe library services for those who are infrequent users or nonusers. We must, however, consider them as potential users. In New York State, for example, outreach is defined as a "program of library services designed to identify, contact, and serve persons who are educationally disadvantaged; members of ethnic or minority groups in need of special library services; unemployed and in need of job placement assistance; living in areas underserved by a library; blind, physically handicapped, aged, or confined in institutions."[3]

Such definitions default to specific categories of users rather than to specific types of collections, programs, and services that can expand the capacity of a library's service delivery plan. Services for specific user groups are often segregated and not perceived in relation to everyday library activities.

In June 2002, the planning committee for an ALA preconference, Different Voices, Common Quest: Adult Literacy and Outreach in Libraries, received a letter from a public library director in the Midwest that took issue with the idea of convening such an event. He asserted that in these times of budgetary and social uncertainty, focus should be steady on the day-to-day services that libraries currently provide—to *regular* users. Outreach is extracurricular for this library leader.

So who is a regular library user? Someone who uses the library frequently? Someone who is fluent in library language and customs? Someone who supports the status quo at the local library?

When viewed as a tag for those who are not regular, outreach sets up a model of "otherness" that seems to diminish the value of the services and the individuals associated with them. Outreach is often defined by group difference without recognizing the similarity of ongoing needs of that group. The concept of *regular library services* consequently denotes an amorphous prototype that is not detailed with social, economic, or personal traits that characterize an individual's quest for knowledge. The result of such separation is that outreach services do not provide access that is equitable to the total population of users. Another concern that arises when outreach is segregated from regular library services is that outreach staff perceive themselves and the services they provide as marginal and expendable. These concerns are voiced at bookmobile, rural library, and outreach meetings by those who are directly involved in service delivery as well as those who administer the libraries where the service takes place. It is understood that "making do" or eliminating services is the norm when budget cuts are threatened. Unfortunately, those being denied services due to budget cuts are often those with a critical need for information about jobs, education, or health care—information that is available at no cost in a library setting.

These perceptions must be addressed when discussing new strategies for equitable service delivery. In the current economy, outreach services are often the first to be cut. The subtext of such practices is that the most important library users are those who choose regular services, and therefore the most important library staff are those who serve those users.

What we advocate in this book is the development and implementation of standards of service that are fair and balanced. This does not mean that you should change or develop new standards, but rather that you should review your service delivery strategies to ensure that all library users and potential users receive the same quality of service. If developing new standards would help achieve this end, then we must get to work!

EQUITY AS OUTREACH

Equitable delivery of library service is a more holistic approach to outreach. Sameness and difference are no longer seen as mutually exclusive but rather as complementary. We can embrace general traits of humanness while recognizing that a multitude of experiences defines and affects individuals and groups. The 2000 census confirmed that each of our communities is diverse, global, and representative of the human condition.

There are 35 million people over the age of 65 in the United States, and about 42 percent of them have some type of disability. About 25 percent of people between 18 and 24 did not graduate from high school. One child in six (11.4 million) lives in poverty. There were 31 million immigrants counted in the census, and about 13.2 million came since 1990. Many of these new Americans have little or no experience with free library services.

The census itself illustrates how our social constructs have become larger and at the same time more specific. New survey questions offer respondents the option of identifying one or more categories to indicate racial identities. New questions were included to learn more about adults over 30 who have primary responsibilities for raising grandchildren or related children under 18 years of age. Questions about persons with disabilities were expanded to find data on specific types of conditions, with different indicators for different age groups.

We also have learned more about literacy and learning, especially for adults, another underserved population in libraries. From the National Adult Literacy Survey of 1992 we know that some 40 to 44 million of the 191 million adults in this country demonstrated the lowest level of prose, document, and quantitative proficiencies (level 1). Another 50 million scored at level 2 proficiency. The survey noted, "Individuals in levels 1 and 2 were much less likely to respond correctly to the more challenging literacy tasks in the assessment . . . they were apt to experience considerable difficulty in performing tasks that required them to integrate or synthesize information from complex or lengthy texts or to perform quantitative tasks that involved two or more sequential operations and in which the individual had to set up the problem."[4] Consider these findings as you review the array of services at your library and the expectations of skills possessed by potential users.

The communities we serve in any type of library are diversely diverse. Many of these diversities are largely invisible (e.g., country of origin, level of education, some disabilities, native language). Regardless, all members of our communities must be able to use the library as they wish and communicate with staff or machines as to their information needs and be successful in their pursuit of knowledge—and thereby be supportive of the library as a social asset. Provision of diverse points of access and delivery of quality services that respond to diverse needs must be the goals of the library profession in the twenty-first century.

OUTREACH, EQUITY, AND ALA

ALA has advocated for services to different, special populations since its inception, taking actions that often challenged its members to rethink the values of their profession. In the early part of the twentieth century ALA committees addressed service delivery issues of immigrants, rural communities, prison populations, and people with visual disabilities. The association effectively lobbied for government support to serve these special populations (e.g., the establishment of the National Library for the Blind and Physically Handicapped in 1931). For many years, ALA advocated for federal funding for construction and support of libraries in rural areas, resulting in the Library Services Act (LSA) of 1956. In 1964, the legislation was expanded to encompass various underserved populations—handicapped, urban poor, seniors, and illiterate.

At the same time, ALA sponsored professional activities for library staff to support social and legislative changes. In 1971, the Committee on Library Service to the Disadvantaged and Unserved was formed. Funding and staff were added to support research, model programs, adult literacy projects, services to Appalachians and American Indian peoples, and services to rural and urban poor. In 1980 the committee became the Office for Library Outreach Services—a line item in ALA's budget. Today this unit is known as the Office for Literacy and Outreach Services (OLOS).

In its role as advocate of services for traditionally underserved populations, OLOS has become a clearinghouse for outreach resources, dedicating websites, conference programs, electronic discussion lists, publications, and external partnerships to support library staff in a variety of settings. ALA President Carla Hayden recognized the unique role of OLOS in her appointment of Satia Marshall Orange to oversee the creation of this volume—a significant new resource in the clearinghouse.

President Hayden called for the profession as a whole to embrace the ideal of equity of access. She wrote, "It is my hope that by planning and working with ALA's units and affiliates, we can fully integrate this issue into the goals and activities of the association as a whole."[5] As an infrastructure of diverse professional interests, all ALA units can provide tools to support library staff as they develop services toward this end. Here are examples of tools available now:

> The Library Instruction Round Table Committee on Adult Learners has developed lists of suggested readings to understand learning style and training resources for adult learners. Some readings discuss specific learning groups, including older adults, English language learners, adults who are learning basic literacy skills, and those with learning disabilities.[6]
>
> Buildliteracy.org, a Web initiative of ALA's Office for Literacy and Outreach Services funded by Verizon, helps library staff access resources to develop literacy coalitions with other local agencies. The site features sections on coalition building, profiles of literacy coalitions, and ways to sustain existing coalitions.
>
> The Technology and Access Committee of the Library and Information Technology Association has prepared an access assessment checklist that includes a detailed section with prompts to assess services in relation to literacy, cultural background, and physical or learning disabilities.[7]

We look forward to the development of similar resources from other ALA units as we work collaboratively to improve our policies and practices.

From Outreach to Equity presents successful models of library practices and policies that support equitable delivery of services in many communities across the country. They are few, but they are mighty and deserve recognition. The models are outcome-based and are organized by types of services that can strengthen users' connections to information:

- Services outside library walls
- Outreach inside the library
- Information technology
- Technical services
- Advocacy
- Staff development

The sections on advocacy and staff development encourage the understanding of the interdependence of internal structures and external realities and illustrate how this relationship affects equitable service delivery.

Libraries can make a difference, and they always have. And librarians can continue to expand their knowledge and skills in order to help their institutions achieve their service goals. We will realize the promise of the Library Bill of Rights to provide "for the interest, information, and enlightenment of all people of the community the library serves."

NOTES

1. American Library Association, Library Bill of Rights, 1948, amended 1961, 1980, and 1996. Available at www.ala.org/Content/NavigationMenu/Our_Association/ Offices/Intellectual_Freedom3/Statements_and_Policies/Intellectual_Freedom2/ Library_Bill_of_Rights.htm.. Accessed 4 December 2003.
2. Carla Hayden, "Presidential Initiative: Equity of Access." Available at www.ala .org/Content/NavigationMenu/Our_Association/Governance/Executive_Board/ Hayden/initatives.htm. Accessed 15 December 2003.
3. New York State Law and Regulations of the Commissioner of Education pertaining to Libraries, Library Systems, Trustees, and Librarians: Title 8, Section 5, L.
4. National Institute for Literacy, "Frequently Asked Questions: How Literate Is the Adult Population?" Available at www.nifl.gov/nifl/faqs.html#literacyrates. Accessed 30 October 2003.
5. Hayden.
6. Adult Learners Resource Center (ALA Library Instruction Round Table). Available at www3.baylor.edu/LIRT/adultlearning.htm. Accessed 20 December 2003.
7. Technology and Access Committee of Library Information and Technology Association, home page. Available at www.lita.org/Content/NavigationMenu/ LITA/LITA_Membership/LITA_Committees/Technology_and_Access_Committee/ Technology_and_Access_Committee.htm. Accessed 20 December 2003.

PART 1

Services outside Library Walls

Jan Meadows
Pikes Peak Library District
Colorado Springs, Colorado

IN THE BEGINNING, OUTREACH USUALLY referred to services that were offered outside the walls of the library building. Librarians have always been concerned with offering services to those not ready or able to come to the library. There were traveling libraries in New York and Michigan in the late 1890s. Children's staff would visit schools and settlement houses to encourage reading. The Works Progress Administration of the 1930s included library demonstration projects. These projects hired library staff to extend services to rural and other underserved populations, often on bookmobiles. State and public libraries created new departments for reaching outside their walls with titles such as extension service, outreach, and special needs department.

In most libraries today, these departments provide one or more of the following services outside their walls: bookmobiles; homebound services;

deposit collections; and service to residential facilities, hospitals, shelters, jails, and target populations. These departments also present demonstrations and programs about library services in community forums.

Libraries must—by their own mandate—provide equitable access to services for everyone. That often means leaving the library and taking the service to underserved populations. There are many barriers to access. The most obvious ones are faced by people with physical disabilities. Developmental disabilities pose other barriers. Age becomes a barrier for the elderly as well as the very young because both need assistance to get to or inside a library. There are geographic barriers for those who live in isolated areas or long distances from a library branch. For children, a busy highway or street between their home and the library becomes a geographic barrier. Social circumstances such as poverty, lack of transportation, inability to speak the language, and illiteracy are barriers for some people. Finally, a simple lack of knowledge about library services keeps many folks from accessing service.

Equitable access needs to be a real part of library service, fully funded in the annual budget and not just supported by grants or other "soft money" that can disappear at any time. Commitment to such services benefits both the library and the community. By reaching out, the library stimulates the discovery of knowledge, provides resources that can improve the quality of life for residents, and promotes intellectual freedom and lifelong learning. These services make the library a part of the community's heart and soul. As such, the library can develop relationships with community members who will aid the library in its future work—a circle of loyal library supporters. And whether we like it or not, our society moves at such high speed that people respond favorably to service that is convenient. It is profitable to both the library and the patrons to have services, such as bookmobiles, that offer quick, easy access.

To start and sustain service outside its walls, a library needs to follow certain steps.

COMMITMENT

It is most important to have the commitment of the director and the library board. They must include outreach/extension services in the library's mission statement *and* budget. By doing this they are demonstrating their belief in and support of equitable service delivery. They must hire or appoint creative, hardworking managers, supervisors, and staff who are also committed to equitable access. Outreach takes dedication, a firm belief in the work, and lots of initiative.

ASSESSMENT/RESEARCH

With staff in place, assessments must be conducted in order to shape the program. First, the library's strengths, weaknesses, and resources need to be evaluated. Then the library needs to identify what segments of the community are unserved or underserved and how library services could benefit them. This can be determined through census records, surveys of community residents and library users, and interviews with leaders of cultural groups and staff of facilities serving target groups, focus groups, or community meetings. As Yolanda Cuesta and Gail McGovern stated at the 2002 ALA Annual Conference, "In gathering community information, it is essential to identify those community connections *not* typically involved in library activities. The most valuable connections are individuals and members of groups who serve as pathways to the heart of a particular segment of the community."[1]

While assessing the needs of the un- or underserved, we should also assess the "gifts" those same groups can offer the library. As John Kretzmann and John McKnight suggest, "Each community boasts a unique combination of assets upon which to build its future. A thorough map of those assets would begin with an inventory of the gifts, skills and capacities of the community's residents."[2] They recommend mapping the assets of citizens' groups, private businesses, and public institutions. The contacts you make in your outreach assessment can be potential partners, so it is advantageous to assess both needs and gifts.

After learning about potential groups to serve and potential partners, the library needs to decide the level of participation it can afford and commit to. There is still a lot of research to do before designing the program. Contact other libraries with services similar to those you want to provide and ask about problems, pitfalls, and successes. Join an electronic discussion group. Read everything. You can never have too much information.

PLANNING

Now it's time to plan. First and foremost, be sure the service has been incorporated into the library's strategic plan. Create clear goals and objectives of service. Make a work plan that has clear action steps. Interview potential partners and contacts you discovered during your assessment and find new ones. Think of every business, church, or community group the target population may come in contact with and how a partnership might be formed with them. Possible partners for outreach services could include literacy groups, meals-on-wheels, senior centers, traveling health care providers, ethnic community centers, cable TV stations, and the housing authority, to name just a few. Once a partnership has been established, be sure to create partnership agreements so that all parties understand their commitments and responsibilities.

MARKETING

Marketing your new service is vital to its success. Carry brochures, bookmobile schedules, and other materials in your car at all times. You never know when you will be somewhere you can post or leave them—a business, church, doctor's office, or post office, for example. Keep in touch with your community relations or public relations department. Knowing their deadlines and preferred format for fliers and brochures will ensure that you get the word out in a timely way. Brainstorm new or different ways to reach the target audience.

- Post signs, similar to those used by real estate companies, on corners and in yards, indicating the time and location of a bookmobile stop in the neighborhood.
- Distribute door hangers for community center programs.
- Send staff in costume to visit neighborhood schools or community centers.

How can your partners help? Can they include information about your service in their mailings? Arm them with the information they need to talk about your service with their clients and customers. They most likely already have a relationship with the people you are trying to reach, and their confidence in your service will be some of the best promotion you can have.

The most important element in marketing is enthusiasm. Be enthusiastic about your service no matter where you are. Enthusiasm is contagious!

In-House Marketing

The success of your outreach program also depends on your interaction with other departments within your library—in-house marketing. Attend other departmental meetings to share what is happening in outreach/extension services. Answer their questions so they can answer patrons' questions about your service. Distribute a bookmobile magnet or a pencil with your department name and phone extension printed on it as a reminder of your service. Provide program schedules to keep at service desks. Let them know how important their help is to you, your staff, and patrons. Send out an in-house e-mail to "All" about a staff person from another department who went the extra mile to help you and your patrons. Send a chocolate bar to a staff member who provided assistance or spread the word about your work. Do what you can to keep your service on the library staff's radar screen so they can answer questions or promote it to patrons.

MAINTENANCE

Once the service is established, you have to maintain and grow it. Review and evaluate it frequently so that you can address problems and build upon strengths. Frontline staff have firsthand experience, so they will have invaluable input. They should know that the supervisor's door—and mind—are always open to them. Supervisors should let their outreach staff know how much they appreciate the effort they expend.

Staff should be encouraged to share experiences for about 10 minutes a day when they return to the home base, while problems and successes are fresh in their minds. It is a great way for them to decompress from the stresses of the day, and these chat times can lead to improvements in processes and service.

Provide as much relevant training as possible for staff. Reference interview training, Internet training, cultural sensitivity training relating to a target group, and customer service training are all relevant to outreach/extension staff. If the library is limited in its ability to send staff members to conferences, make sure the educational opportunities selected will give them the most information in their field and the library the most for its training dollar. For example, send bookmobile staff to the Great American Bookmobile Conference. It will give them the opportunity to share their expertise with others who are doing the same work and to develop new approaches to their own service. Training will reenergize them and give them the tools they need.

Patrons know better what they need than we do, so provide them with ways to give you feedback. "How are we doing?" or "What would you like?"

fliers or bookmarks give them a written format that facilitates input. Staff who work with patrons on a regular basis should be trained to listen and learn about how to improve services. The supervisor's site visits for one-on-one chats with patrons affirm the library's interest in their perspectives.

Keep in continual contact with partners to let them know that their help is valuable to you. Send an occasional thank-you card. To foster teamwork, consider having an annual or biannual meeting or informal gatherings with outreach staff and the partner's staff. Be sure to highlight your partner in fliers and brochures about your service or programs. Send a copy of your annual report or statistics to your partners so they can see how your service is growing. Basically, just keep them in the loop so they can see how they have been instrumental in the success of your service.

In the following pages you will find excellent models of many kinds of service outside library walls. Read about an awesome techmobile (equipped with on-line computer stations as well as a print collection) that serves a multicultural population; a library that redesigned the administration of deposit collections to maximize its resources and service; and a bookmobile that serves preschoolers as well as teachers and caregivers. The New Mexico State Library reminds us of the support that state libraries provide to foster professional development and information services for end users. We hope all of the articles will inspire you to reach out to the underserved in your community and to build your own unique programs to facilitate the equitable delivery of services.

NOTES

1. Yolanda Cuesta and Gail McGovern, "Rural Library Communities." Presented at American Library Association Annual Conference, June 17, 2002. Available at www.ala.org/ala/olos/olosprograms/preconferences/rural_communities.pdf. Accessed 19 April 2004.
2. John P. Kretzmann and John McKnight, *Building Communities from the Inside Out: A Path toward Finding and Mobilizing a Community's Assets* (Evanston, Ill.: Asset-Based Community Development Institute, Northwestern University, 1993), 6.

Library Elderly Outreach Project

Jane Karp
St. Johns County Public Library System
St. Augustine, Florida

ST. JOHNS COUNTY PUBLIC LIBRARY SYSTEM hosts a number of special programs for seniors as part of the Library Elderly Outreach (LEO) Project. The outreach librarian and one library assistant conduct the programs in senior facilities across our service area.

Our patrons are the senior and disabled residents of St. Johns County, Florida, and their caretakers. We visit all 31 of the licensed facilities in the county twice a month. These include nursing homes, senior residential or retirement communities, assisted living facilities, memory centers, Council on Aging programs, and adult day care centers.

The main feature of LEO is a complete library on wheels, a van designed specifically for seniors. It has a low floor chassis with a wheelchair ramp that conforms to standards set out in the Americans with Disabilities Act. Four book carts are secured in the van for transport and then detached and wheeled into facilities where patrons are unable to come out to the van.

The van houses a collection that includes everything from the hottest best-sellers to classics in fiction and nonfiction. Most of the books, magazines, and newspapers are large print, but we also carry regular-print items, including the

New York Times. We have books on CD and audiocassette, VHS and DVD movies, music CDs, audiocassette players, and magnifiers. Staff provide reader's advisory services, answer reference queries, handle requests for interlibrary loans or items to purchase, and issue library cards. There are materials available from the Division of the Blind, Community Hospice of Northeast Florida, and United Way as well as voter registration forms and library information.

LEO also helps seniors connect with technology. A 2002 Library Services and Technology Act grant enabled us to place 10 computers in senior facilities. In 2003 we began holding classes to teach seniors basic computer skills, including Internet and e-mail usage and library catalog instructions. These lessons are posted on our library web page under Online Courses so students can review what they learned at their leisure. By popular demand we have expanded our classes to include word processing, spreadsheets, and digital photography. With the help of our volunteers, mostly teens and college students, we have taught well over 2,000 seniors to use computers.

To demonstrate how useful computers can be, we developed our own version of the *Antiques Roadshow* program. Participants bring in an antique or collectible and we go on-line to find its history, including when and where it was made, by whom, its dollar value, and what makes it unique. We then access the auction houses' Web pages to determine its market value. One patron sold a meteorite that fell in his field for $250,000. Lately, these Roadshow programs have been packed!

We also show seniors how to use First Coast Help, St. Johns County's social service database maintained by the library system. This directory lists programs and services available in health care, education, child care, referral, emergency, employment, food, housing, recreation, and other areas.

Life on the road allows us to conduct a variety of programs in the facilities we visit. We use Bi-Folkal activity kits for senior and intergenerational programs, themed and holiday programs, visual and audio recognition programs, chapter readings, LEO mysteries, and LEO memoirs. Our newest offering is the Veterans History Project, a partnership with the American Folklife Center in the Library of Congress. We are training volunteers to interview military veterans to collect their stories as a way of honoring them for their service to the nation.

InfoBUS: Serving Immigrant and Refugee Populations

Damone Virgilio
Memphis–Shelby County Public Library
Memphis, Tennessee

IN THE 1990S, MEMPHIS, LIKE MANY OTHER U.S. cities, experienced significant increases in immigration. In response to the challenge of serving these growing communities, Memphis-Shelby County Public Library & Information Center launched InfoBUS, a mobile branch library dedicated to serving the county's immigrant and refugee population. This is a short history of InfoBUS.

When we began to strategize for InfoBUS service, we realized that we would need to find out how and where to meet our target audience. We accomplished this by meeting with agencies that provided services to immigrants and refugees. Library personnel began to serve on boards of these agencies, which provided invaluable information to help develop services for these distinct communities.

InfoBUS service began on September 9, 1999. The 40-foot bus featured colorful graphics with the words "Library" and "Welcome" in Spanish, Chinese, and Vietnamese. It offered eight computers with Internet access as well as English as a second language (ESL) collections and foreign language collections. Staff included three bilingual librarians and a full-time driver/circulation clerk. In our first year, InfoBUS encountered nearly 6,000 customers, mostly at festivals, community fairs, church ESL programs, and ESL centers in city schools.

The library learned a great deal about the obstacles affecting service delivery. The most obvious barrier was language. We needed reading materials in several different languages; staff who could communicate effectively with diverse groups; and signs, forms, and documents in a variety of languages. We researched collections of other library systems, interviewed InfoBUS customers and area service providers, and consulted with various publishers in order to establish a baseline collection. Our staff development department initiated basic and intermediate Spanish conversation classes. We relied on library staff and community contacts to translate important forms and signs.

Our first 18 months of InfoBUS service confirmed the need for the types of information and services we provided, as our usage increased by about 30 percent. However, we recognized the need to systematize services to the international community throughout Memphis and Shelby County. We invited ALA's Library Administration and Management Association to conduct a workshop on serving diverse communities. The two-day training encouraged our administration and public service personnel to look critically at the services the library provided and to create a process for improving those services throughout the system.

After the workshop, we wanted to survey the community to identify needs and establish service priorities. Our diversity committee created a survey tool and polled 17 international community leaders, including clergy, health care providers, social service administrators, educators, and government representatives. Primary information needs were language development, employment information, and information on how to access health care and education. The primary barriers to meeting those needs were lack of multilingual resources and lack of awareness of services.

Survey respondents applauded the library's efforts, notably outreach via InfoBUS, positioning of bilingual staff at key access points, and the development of foreign language collections. They also noted the need for more resources, visibility, bilingual staff, and targeted outreach. In essence, the respondents justified the need to expand InfoBUS services.

The InfoBUS currently averages about 40 stops per month, and it is difficult to juggle requests for service. There are not enough staff members or hours to serve every location and have a significant impact. Our goal is to acquire an additional unit designed for children's services, with ample storage for art supplies, a fiction and nonfiction juvenile collection, and bilingual services for children in the Memphis City Schools ESL program and other agencies served.

One notable partnership has emerged with ESL instructors in the Memphis City Schools. The InfoBUS children's librarian is learning about curriculum, activities, and resources used in ESL classes and will develop a collection to support the curriculum. InfoBUS staff will also create children's programs that support English language development, offer parent and teacher materials that supplement classroom materials, and reinforce lessons and activities presented to students and their families.

The support of the administration of Memphis-Shelby County Public Library and Information Center underscores that InfoBUS is part of the larger system. As InfoBUS staff members learn from our community, we must share this information with the rest of the system so that we deliver consistent services. As we develop new practices to improve services, we must also communicate effectively with other library personnel. Our commitment to providing excellent service to the international community must be reflected in every branch and at every service point in the library system. Then the library will indeed have something for everyone.

Serving Homeless People: Partnering with Shelters and Transitional Homes

Lisa A. Canavan
Multnomah County Library
Portland, Oregon

IN OCTOBER 1987, OREGON'S MULTNOMAH County Library initiated a program "to serve those who may temporarily be in the area to use the food and shelter programs, to provide limited social service referrals, and to provide limited reference service." A part-time coordinator worked with an advisory committee to establish a storefront location in downtown Portland as a safe and comfortable place for homeless people to read during the day. The Old Town Reading Room opened in 1988 with a Library Services and Construction Act grant of $26,400. Volunteers staffed the reading room. After the grant expired, the library assumed the operational costs, including coordinator's salary, rent, utilities, cleaning service, and a small book budget.

By 1992, a local agency survey ranked the Old Town Reading Room as the third most frequently used agency among the homeless and low-income population. Patrons did not need identification to check out materials, and the return rate was comparable with most branch libraries. A 1996 report noted that the 980-square-foot space had steady patronage, with an average of 70 people per day and approximately 2,038 visits per month.

Over time, the Multnomah County Library realized that the reading room was not the most effective way to serve the changing homeless population. Although a few women, minorities, and youth used it, the main population served was older white men. The operating costs had more than doubled to $74,687, which included a security guard to respond to persistent problem patrons. The return rate for materials had declined precipitously. In 1996, a library team recommended closing the reading room and establishing deposit collections at specific agencies. On June 1, 1997, the Old Town Reading Room closed, and its materials were dispersed.

But Multnomah County Library was committed to serving homeless people. In November 1997 it established the program that now serves homeless shelters and transitional homes for women, men, and youth throughout Multnomah County—not only Portland's downtown. Reading materials are provided to more than 30 shelter and transitional programs, 60 percent of which include service to children and teens.

Most of the materials distributed are discards from branch collections and paperback donations. The collections also include undeliverable magazines from the post office. A part-time program coordinator conducts initial and follow-up interviews with shelter staff to determine their typical population and material preferences. We include a request sheet with each delivery so staff can let us know when their patrons' needs change. We have a small budget that allows us to purchase books targeted to specific segments of this population. About 40 percent of the purchases in 2003 were children's books in English and Spanish. Adult Spanish-language and African American-themed books were other major purchases. We also purchase heavily in the areas of addiction/recovery, job hunting, abuse, parenting, early childhood literacy, and health.

Volunteers deliver collections and pick up returned books monthly. Agencies can use and distribute materials as they see fit. They don't need to be concerned if residents take the books when they leave or books become damaged. We have about a 25 percent to 30 percent return rate, with these materials going back into program circulation.

Young county residents contribute to the shelter outreach program through our summer reading program when they donate the value of their prize award to purchase children's books. We also provide opportunities for shelter residents to participate in broader library programs. In 2003 the Multnomah County Library had its inaugural "Everybody Reads" program, where local residents read the same book. All the shelters received paperback copies of the book. Several requested multiple copies for reading groups, and one or two requested videos that would be viewed and discussed on-site.

Systemwide newsletters and brochures promoting library services and programs are included in all deliveries. Our ultimate mission is to make everyone feel comfortable about using library services.

Deposit Collections: Streamlining Procedures for Better Service

Patricia Linhoff
Hennepin County Library
Minnetonka, Minnesota

DEPOSIT COLLECTIONS ARE COORDINATED programs that place library materials in settings that may be preferred or exclusive access points for some library users. The outreach department at Hennepin County Library in suburban Minneapolis supports 52 deposit collections at a variety of agencies throughout the area, including nursing homes, independent and assisted living sites for seniors, and rehabilitation centers. Our newest partners are four learning centers serving new Americans. The waiting list for services grows as new senior sites and new immigrant communities proliferate in our service area.

In 1995, coordination of the collections was centralized in the Hennepin County Library's outreach department. Dedicating staff and resources to support the program resulted in a more holistic and efficient service. One of the keys to success has been to circulate boxes of materials rather than single items. The colorful plastic boxes contain materials of a specific type or format. There are 335 large-print boxes, 40 regular-print, and 33 learning center boxes, each with 15 items selected according to a profile. The boxes for learning centers include audiotapes for learning English, citizenship information, high school equivalency materials, resources for teaching English as a second language, slower-paced talking books, and a variety of nonfiction.

Each site receives from three to eight boxes, each containing a packing sheet that lists title, author, book number, and bar code number. The site lets us know via the packing slip if anything is missing or damaged when the collection is returned. We simply scan the box, replenish any missing items, check the missing items out to the site's card, and move that box back to our inventory. It is also easy to track the movement of any box of materials.

Collections are replaced six times per year. New materials are routinely ordered by collection management services according to a profile of authors and genres developed in collaboration with the agencies. Each item arrives in outreach fully processed with the special status "OR/NA" (outreach/not available), so it cannot be trapped for system holds.

This efficiency in the physical administration of the deposit collections frees the staff to provide an array of supplemental services to our clients. We offer reference and reader's advisory services by phone and e-mail. We send special requests to readers at the deposit collection site. We give book talks and training on accessing on-line information. We also support book clubs by suggesting titles, gathering multiple copies of a title, and locating information about the author. Six times a year we send partner agencies the *At Home Reader*, a reader's advisory newsletter about new books and library programs. Frequent site visits and phone calls keep the lines of communication open.

Hennepin County Library's deposit collection program brings quality library services to residents of nursing homes, rehabilitation centers, and senior living facilities. Our streamlined procedures allow staff to focus less on gathering materials and more on building collections, relationships, and community.

Bookmobile Service to Preschool Children and Caregivers

Theresa Gemmer
Everett Public Library
Everett, Washington

THE EVERETT PUBLIC LIBRARY'S BOOKMOBILE outreach to preschool children started 15 years ago. Because many preschoolers do not have the opportunity to visit a library when both parents work and have busy schedules, the bookmobile brings the library to them. Each month during the school year we visit more than 50 preschool groups, including Head Start classrooms, preschool programs, and day care centers. We serve about nine hundred children per month.

The bookmobile goes to each site and parks in a safe and accessible place. The librarian goes into the center to conduct a story time for the children and caregivers, including fingerplays, music, and songs. In addition to entertaining the children, the story time demonstrates to caregivers how to hold the children's interest by choosing appropriate materials and reading with expression. Modeling story time technique is extremely valuable. A caregiver at one center noticed that I held the book so children could see the pictures and said she would try that next time. Caretakers learn about new titles and classic favorites. They are given handouts that include the books and the fingerplays or songs used in the session.

After story time, the children and caregivers come out to the bookmobile and choose books to take into the center. The caregivers are assisted in choosing books to read to the children and to enhance their curriculum. Some assistance is passive—displaying new or topical books in a noticeable spot, for example. When assisting a caregiver in choosing materials, we explain why we are selecting certain titles. The bookmobile librarian might say, "For toddlers, we want to choose books with bright, clear pictures and only a few words per page," or "These 'let's-read-and-find-out' science books are meant to be read aloud to preschoolers."

We stock a collection of teacher resource materials. The most popular are books that contain curriculum units with lesson plans and activities that can be used immediately. Although each center establishes its own lesson plans, there are always common themes. The bookmobile collection contains curriculum kits on popular topics such as fall, winter holidays, sea life, and cultural awareness. The kits include several read-aloud books, an idea book, audiovisual materials, and sometimes puzzles or other realia.

Other than support materials for caregivers, the bookmobile is exclusively for children, stocking a variety of picture books, simple nonfiction, and music for children. The arrangement of shelves makes simple nonfiction readily accessible, and this category accounts for about one-third of the materials chosen by preschoolers. Dinosaurs, trucks, ballet, trains, cats, dogs, sharks, folktales, and assorted animal books, especially those with photographs rather than drawings, are the most popular.

Caregivers are encouraged to call ahead with curriculum requests so that staff can bring additional books from the library's collection. It is an ongoing challenge to establish this line of communication. Some centers see a large staff turnover, so new teachers always need to be made aware of the support the library can offer. Where staff is more stable and familiar with our services, teachers call us or send their requests by e-mail. When there is an established curriculum, we ask for a copy of the plan and then bring items prechecked to the center to enhance their lessons.

A recent study of the significance of books in early education concluded that "childcare centers are ill-equipped to provide the kinds of activities and practices necessary for children to engage in reading and become literate, despite calls to the contrary. Consequently, those children from low-income families who are most in need of access to print will not find a safety net in childcare centers."[1] Libraries can help fill the "book gap" by reaching out to children and caregivers in child care settings. We library professionals must use our knowledge and skills to support young children with the books they need to grow and thrive.

NOTE

1. Susan B. Neuman et al., *Access for All: Closing the Book Gap for Children in Early Education* (Newark, Del.: International Reading Association, 2001).

Outreach to Prisons: Connecting Inmates and Public Library Services

Glennor Shirley
Correctional Education Libraries
Maryland State Department of Education
Baltimore, Maryland

THERE ARE MORE THAN TWO MILLION PRISONers in federal, state, and local jails. About 95 percent of the state prisoners will be released back into their communities. Some 1.5 million children have a parent in prison. Do public libraries offer services to ex-offenders returning to their communities or to incarcerated parents and their children? Many do, and there are some innovative programs that underscore the value of such services.

Prisons are the inmates' communities, and prisoners have the same kinds of information needs as citizens outside the fence. Maryland Correctional Education Libraries (MCEL) operate like community libraries, providing information and services to meet the lifelong learning and recreational reading needs of the inmates. Maryland has 13 major prison libraries. The libraries have career centers to provide transition information for some 15,000 inmates released from Maryland prisons each year.

Ex-offenders need information on housing, homeless shelters, drug addiction centers, jobs and careers, licensing and apprenticeship, health care, credit, parenting, and domestic relationships. They rarely think of going to their public libraries to get this information.

MCEL developed a CD-ROM tutorial, *Discovering the Internet@Your Library*, to teach inmates how to use the Internet and to promote public libraries as important places to get information on a variety of topics. Of 1,663 inmates completing the tutorial to date, 1,560 indicated they would visit the public libraries for their job search needs when they returned to society. A few of them telephoned their children to encourage them to visit the public libraries.

Public libraries can partner with correctional facilities to connect inmates with the richness of information and services available to them and their families. The Enoch Pratt Free Library worked with MCEL to connect ex-offenders to career resources available at the public library. The Enoch Pratt Free Library job center specialist conducted a workshop titled "I'm Out, Now Where Is the Help?" at the Correctional Education Association that highlighted public library collections, programs, and Internet resources that are available to ex-offenders who are seeking information on GED, jobs, resume writing, or other practical concerns.

Another innovative effort developed in partnership with the Enoch Pratt Free Library is Family Literacy@Your Library, a program that encourages inmates to read with their children. At the Maryland House of Corrections, a maximum security prison, we trained 12 inmates to be storytellers and readers. The children's library coordinator of the Howard County Library conducted a session on selecting appropriate children's books, and children's staff from the Enoch Pratt Free Library conducted sessions on storytelling, selecting books, using props, and interacting with children. Inspired by the seemingly effortless storytelling techniques of the library staff, the men overcame their self-consciousness and with increasing enthusiasm have planned the monthly Family Literacy@Your Library events. Once a month in the prison visiting room, children, their caregivers, and the incarcerated parents read together. In the summer, families participated in the Blast Off to Reading summer reading game. One grandfather who has been incarcerated for 35 years and admits he had never heard of *Curious George* now encourages his granddaughter to go to the library. The children's department of the Enoch Pratt Free Library developed a rotating deposit collection of 60 juvenile books to offer the men a wider selection of stories to read with their children.

There are many other ways public libraries can support this underserved population. For example, our prison librarians operate as one-person managers and might benefit from the programming expertise of their public library counterparts. The Library Services to Prisoners Forum of the Association of

Specialized and Cooperative Library Agencies addresses this issue. You can also check out the website MCEL developed to assist our librarians: http://ce .msde.state.md.us/library/library.htm.

Tribal Libraries Program of the New Mexico State Library

Dana John
New Mexico State Library
Albuquerque, New Mexico

THE TRIBAL LIBRARIES PROGRAM OF THE NEW Mexico State Library is an innovative service that offers specialized library development to tribal communities on a statewide basis. The mission of the program is to promote and support information access in tribal communities with emphasis on current technology and tribal library development. The Tribal Libraries Program serves nearly 139,000 Pueblo, Apache, and Navajo community members in New Mexico. It employs two full-time consultants and has a training and outreach center located on the Navajo Nation in Crownpoint.

The Tribal Libraries Program was developed in 1994 in response to a call by State Senator Leonard Tsosie for improved library services and Internet access in New Mexico tribal communities. The New Mexico State Library rose to the challenge and created the Tribal Libraries Program. Funded for three years by the state legislature, the program initially provided computer equipment in tribal libraries and information centers, technology support, Internet access, and technology and Internet training workshops. In 1998, permanent funding of $270,000 per year was allocated to the New Mexico State Library to ensure the continuation and growth of the program.

Today, the Tribal Libraries Program consists of a direct grant program, technology training and support, consulting services, technical services support, and other services for tribal communities. Two full-time consultants serve 22 Native American communities in New Mexico by offering individual on-site consultation on all topics, including technology, policies and planning, programming, and best library practices.

The direct grant program helps to improve library services for tribal communities with existing libraries. Fifteen tribal libraries from Apache, Pueblo, and Navajo communities applied for and received direct grants in 2002–3. Based on the needs of their communities, the tribal libraries used these grants for collection development, programming, furniture, computers, software, and a speaker series. Several special grants were also given to organizations that support the mission of the program. The Indigenous Language Institute and the Navajo Nation received funding for language instruction publications and web hosting and domain names.

The Crownpoint Training & Outreach Center was established in 1997 as a branch of the New Mexico State Library. It has 7,500 volumes and a specialized multimedia Native American collection that is available to the public. A full-time outreach librarian provides technology training, handles interlibrary loan requests, and answers reference inquiries for members of the Navajo Nation who live in New Mexico.

Support from the Bill & Melinda Gates Foundation's Native American Access to Technology Program enables the Tribal Libraries Program to offer other training to tribal program staff and community members. Based on local need, workshops have focused on Microsoft Office, Internet research, e-commerce web design, and self-published bilingual books. The foundation also collaborates with the Tribal Libraries Program in the ongoing automation of 15 tribal libraries' collections. Tribal librarians receive on-site assistance with weeding collections and with on-line cataloging.

Words on Wheels and Traveling Library Center: Staffing to Optimize Services

Jeannie Dilger-Hill
King County Library System
Issaquah, Washington

KING COUNTY LIBRARY SYSTEM, WHICH SUR-
rounds the city of Seattle, comprises approximately 2,000 square miles, with
a staff of more than a thousand and a service population of some one million
residents. The library system supports a focused outreach program for seniors and the disabled with two services: the Words on Wheels homebound
service and the Traveling Library Center lobby service.[1]

The Words on Wheels program delivers materials to patrons who have
difficulty walking, driving, carrying books, or seeing titles on shelves and
who expect to need help for at least four months. We visit individual homes,
adult family homes, and adult day care centers.

People learn about our service in a variety of ways. There is no formal
application required to participate. Staff members take contact information
over the phone and talk with patrons about their reading preferences. This
method prevents well-meaning friends or family members from signing up a
patron without his or her consent.

There are currently about 350 individuals on the Words on Wheels service who are visited by staff or volunteers once a month. Volunteers are trained

and operate out of their nearest library branch. A staff liaison will touch base regularly with volunteers and branch staff to make sure all is going well.

Words on Wheels patrons are designated as "homebound" in our library circulation system. The homebound module tracks what patrons have read previously and alerts staff if patrons try to check out an item they have already had.

The Traveling Library Center visits individuals living in nursing homes, assisted living communities, and retirement facilities. This service uses cargo trucks with a rear lift to load six carts of books (regular and large-print), books on tape, music CDs, videos, and DVDs. We also have a smaller "pop-top"-style vehicle that holds only three carts.

The Traveling Library Center visits approximately 150 facilities in the King County area once a month for 30 to 60 minutes each. Carts are pushed into a lobby or library and patrons check out, return, renew, and pick up requests. Circulation is currently recorded by portable communications devices (telxons), which scan bar codes and batch the information for download later. After our lobby service is finished, staff members take carts around to nursing home residents to deliver and pick up materials and to allow them to browse.

At the beginning of this focused outreach program, staff members were assigned to one of the two services. Over time we learned that patrons transition from one service to another. For example, if a Traveling Library Center site has fewer than six visitors, we will cancel stops at that site and move patrons to the Words on Wheels service. We came to understand that training staff to deliver both services makes for better continuity for both the library system and our patrons. It increases staff's familiarity with procedures and practices so they can answer patrons' questions about both services and fill in for each other when necessary.

At this time, we have 11 staff members (9 full time) dedicated to this outreach program. Our current staffing strategies have improved customer service.

NOTE

1. For more information about the Words on Wheels service or the Traveling Library Center, see www.kcls.org/tlc/tlcsvcs/cfm.

PART 2

Outreach inside the Library

Rhea Brown Lawson
Detroit Public Library
Detroit, Michigan

THIS CHAPTER FOCUSES ON OUTREACH PRO-
grams and services that are provided inside the library building. When one
thinks of library outreach, the perception is usually of staff providing services
beyond the library's walls. The programs and services represented in this
chapter have been designed to attract and provide library access to people of
diverse backgrounds, ages, and abilities. All were developed to meet a demonstrated need among an underserved population within a library's community.

The notion of *outreach* programs and services still evokes stark differences in our individual and professional philosophies. The presumption still
prevails in librarydom that outreach is not *real* library work and, thus, many
services and programs we know as outreach are often short-circuited and may
even be set up to fail because of lack of sound organizational commitment

and support. Time and experience have revealed that without support from the leadership of an organization, outreach programs and services will be discontinued after their special funding is exhausted. This is true even when there is a demonstrated need for the service; strong community participation; and qualified administrative staff to handle planning, oversight, implementation, and evaluation.

Many public outreach services and programs, such as adult literacy, services to seniors, programs for new Americans, teens, or children and adults with special needs, begin and end as demonstration projects. The objective of a demonstration project is to use outside funding, or "soft money," to plan, implement, and evaluate a new service or program—most often targeted to an underserved or potential customer base. Such programs are typically funded for a year or two to determine if they meet the needs of the targeted population. In principle, if the demonstration project is successful, the library will incorporate it into its service delivery plan. In practice, however, most demonstration projects are left to die on the proverbial vine due to lack of organizational nourishment.

I have seen this scenario played out many times throughout my 30-plus years as a librarian, scholar, and library administrator. As a profession, we have sent mixed messages to our publics. We reach out to targeted groups and welcome them into the library with relevant services for two or three years, or for as long as the grant lasts, and then we let them go. We promote the library as the people's university—a place of learning and information that is free and welcoming to people from all walks of life to use to enhance their lives. For what people do we exist? Whose lives do we want to enhance? Maybe the answer to this question is clearer than we care to admit.

The increasing number of immigrants and projections of rapidly changing demographics throughout the nation have moved the library profession to search for ways to respond to the drums of change, with the requisite need to reexamine our organizational service philosophies. I hope we can develop new and enduring ways to address these changes as we work to provide equitable library access. Perhaps some clues for moving forward in this vein can be found in the demonstration projects that have survived beyond the specially funded demonstration period. By institutionalizing these projects, library leaders will clearly demonstrate the library's role in our communities in ways that clearly embrace our diverse constituent groups.

I am honored to have as my responsibility for this publication the identification of outreach programs and services that operate inside library buildings. It is critical to note that library administrators have incorporated these services into core operations even though their facilities often exist in strained or uncertain budgetary environments. Because each library has its own fiscal realities, these programs enjoy varying levels of support. There exists in each case, however, an unwavering organizational commitment to meeting demonstrated "nontraditional" service needs.

There are many examples of successful outreach programs inside the library—I call them demonstration project survivors. I asked the managers of eight such programs around the country to share their success stories. I am sure you will agree that they all represent real library work that fosters equitable library access. The absolute success for the profession, however, will be realized when we reach a point where words like "outreach," "special," and "nontraditional" will not be used to describe programs like the ones shared here.

The Child's Place: Inclusive Services for Children with Special Needs

Carrie Banks
Brooklyn Public Library
Brooklyn, New York

BROOKLYN PUBLIC LIBRARY LAUNCHED ITS Child's Place for Children with Special Needs in 1987 to enable children with disabilities to go to the library, just like their peers without disabilities. The Child's Place makes library service accessible to Brooklyn's 67,000 to 82,000 children with physical, cognitive, sensory, emotional, behavioral, and learning disabilities. It is a simple but revolutionary concept that predated the Americans with Disabilities Act by three years. This program has been sustained for 16 years, through three library administrations, affirming the library's mission of serving all the people of Brooklyn.

The Child's Place is based on the principles of multiple intelligences and universal design. Multiple intelligences theory posits that people have seven different intelligences and seven corresponding learning styles that are separate but interdependent.[1] We try to tap many intelligences and learning styles in each program. Universal design refers to the creation of products and environments that can be used by anyone without the need for adaptation.[2] We plan our programs to be fully accessible to all children.

Programs at the Child's Place are inclusive—they are for children with and without disabilities. We offer weekly drop-in programs for children birth to age 12. All programs are literature-based. Even our play programs and gardening activities start with stories. Program content is chosen to be interesting to children with developmental disabilities as well as typically developing children. Storytelling is supplemented with related readings, puppets, music, and movement activities to bring the stories alive for all types of learners. We provide adaptive scissors and precut templates as well as standard scissors and blank paper for craft projects. Our collection includes print, audio, large-print, Braille, board-book, and hi-lo formats so that all children have access to library material. In addition to drop-in programs, we offer special education class visits, hospital readings, parenting workshops, and internships for teens with disabilities.

Other practices at the Child's Place also support inclusiveness. Weekday programs start at 4:30 p.m. to allow for the longer commutes of special education students. When there is no staff available to sign, outside interpreters are provided. Our volunteers include students with Down syndrome, autism, and learning disabilities.

The success of the Child's Place rests on the commitment of the library and the partnerships it has formed with agencies in the disability community. All library departments are involved with the program.

- Friends and Volunteer Services help design programs and recruit volunteers.
- Marketing adapts publicity materials to the needs of our low-vision patrons.
- Collection Development orders the formats we need.
- The Foundation Office works to secure private and government grants.
- Children's service specialists are trained to work with children with special needs.

This systemwide commitment allows us to integrate special services throughout the library. We maintain a core of services and collections at our center and five satellite sites; we provide less-intensive services and materials in all other branches.

Community partnerships help connect children and their families with library services. We work with traditional partners such as schools and with nontraditional partners such as early intervention and therapeutic nurseries, the county's Mental Retardation/Developmental Disabilities Council, and parent support groups. The library plays an important role in the development of inclusive services throughout the community. Our staff teach staff in recreational institutions such as the botanic garden, the zoo, and museums how to develop inclusive services.

It takes commitment to serve the 13,000 children and 10,000 adults we served last year. The library and the disability community are invested in supporting inclusive recreation services and expanding the opportunity for children with special needs. By combining our resources and our creativity we have enriched and will continue to enrich the lives of children with and without disabilities in Brooklyn.

NOTES

1. Thomas Armstrong, *Seven Kinds of Smart: Identifying and Developing Your Many Intelligences* (New York: Penguin, 1993).
2. Trace Research & Development Center, College of Engineering, University of Wisconsin-Madison, "Designing a More Usable World—for All." Available at http://trace.wisc.edu/world. Accessed 12 December 2003.

Assistive Technology Collection: Serving People with Disabilities

Marylou Tuckwiller
Lee County (FL) Library System
Fort Myers, Florida

THE LEE COUNTY LIBRARY SYSTEM PROVIDES a range of services to support older adults and persons with disabilities. We are especially proud of our assistive technology collection. With support from a variety of grants over the years and a generous bequest from a patron, a rudimentary collection of magnifiers and low-tech items has grown to a collection of more than 200 devices. The library system continues to purchase the newest technology to help persons with disabilities. The collection consists of a variety of devices to assist persons with low vision or hearing loss, including a selection of games (e.g., Chinese checkers or backgammon) that are magnified for use by persons with low vision, and devices that can be used to simplify everyday life activities.

Our collection is distinctive in two ways. First of all, each of these assistive devices may be checked out with a library card for two weeks. This gives patrons a chance to use the devices at home, on trips, in stores, or wherever necessary to make sure that the device is able to meet their needs—a "try-before-you-buy" experience. In addition to all the low-tech devices such as magnifiers, liquid level indicators, reachers, and big-button telephones or remote controls, patrons with low vision have a choice of six different types of electronic magnification devices. Some of them can connect to a television and magnify text or images onto the TV screen. For those patrons with hearing loss, there are TTYs (text telephones that transmit written words rather than sound), a voice carryover phone that has a port to accommodate a large visual display unit so that incoming messages are displayed in inch-high letters on a 20-inch screen. We also have a compact text telephone that can be used when traveling. There are several types of personal listening devices, such as TV ears (transmitters with headsets to send sound from televisions), and visual alert signalers. For people who have difficulty projecting their voice, there is a device that will speak any message that is typed into it.

A second unique feature of our assistive technology collection is that users can access a large-print catalog with pictures and descriptions of each device it contains. The first catalog was produced in 1995 with support from a Library Services and Technology Act grant. The third revised edition of our *Catalog of Assistive Devices for Older Adults and Person with Disabilities* will be printed soon. The print catalog is available for free at any library in the Lee County Library System or on-line at www.leecounty.com/library/progserv/ssvcs/ad2002.htm.

The collection itself is housed at the Lee County Talking Books Library, where the staff will give visitors a hands-on experience with any of the assistive devices. The staff conduct many outreach presentations yearly for staff and residents in assisted living facilities, church and civic groups, and at health fairs. These programs include an introduction to the talking books service and a demonstration of assistive devices from the collection.

There are also devices available to patrons to use in our libraries. Larger libraries have wheelchairs for visitors, and all libraries in the Lee County Library System have closed captioned televisions, Pocketalkers (compact amplifiers with microphones to help users participate in our library programs), text telephones, magnifiers, and computers with adaptive software for use in the library. Access to these devices, in or outside the library, helps our users stay connected.

Family Language Kit Program: Connecting with Immigrant Families

Helen Benoit
Hamilton Public Library
Hamilton, Ontario

THE FAMILY LANGUAGE KIT PROGRAM WAS developed by the Hamilton Public Library to promote reading, language development, and library use for new immigrants.

The language kits are part of a family literacy initiative designed to help immigrant families break down language and cultural barriers. Over several years, with the support of many partners, the library has created more than 100 dual-language kits in 15 languages. The kits contain a variety of engaging print and nonprint materials that are fun to share and promote language use and play. Kits focus on themes such as nutrition, safety, health, and the neighborhood. The kits are available in the branches, and most of the picture books are dual language (home language plus English). By providing dual-language materials, we enable families to learn English together.

The language kits grew out of an appreciation of the diversity of the Hamilton area. As a library system serving the whole community, we wanted to introduce books and the library in a respectful way. Our intent was to enlist parents as participants and partners in promoting literacy. Mothers with young children were targeted for special attention because as primary caregivers they have fewer opportunities for outside community connections and language learning experiences. Literacy studies have shown that parents will do things for their children that they won't do for themselves.

We struggled with what materials to purchase and how to involve our intended users. Our partnerships with the Community Action Program for Children, the Parents Helping Parents Program, and the City of Hamilton Social and Public Health Services were essential to the success of the project. Public Health Services hires and trains resource parents to introduce newcomer families to community resources. The library involved these resource parents in testing, translating, and promoting the kits. They are active literacy partners and have incorporated a visit to the local library as part of their community orientation program for newcomers.

All of the materials in the kits have been tested and retested. The resource parents take the kits with them when they visit new immigrant families. They evaluate the contents together and fill out evaluation forms that ask simple, specific questions. Before a kit can circulate, we are sure that the translations are accurate and the material is interesting and fun to read. We also know that the materials are culturally sensitive and appropriate. Testing was a long, slow process, and there were some surprises. A number of the books that we considered visually dull were especially valued by the families. The mothers in the test groups were delighted to be able to share retellings of folktales that they remembered from their childhood. By involving families in the testing process, we generated enthusiasm for the family literacy initiative. The best advertising is word of mouth, and the families who participated in the evaluation process brought other families to the library and proudly pointed out "their kits."

We used some of our regular suppliers for items such as puppets and picture dictionaries, but dual-language materials were initially hard to find. Our regular sources didn't carry the items in the languages we needed. Although access to dual-language materials has improved, publishing still seems to lag a year or two behind immigration trends. The resource parents provided valuable assistance by translating several picture books into languages that were unavailable but desperately needed.

Although the family language kits were initially funded through grants and donations, the library is committed to providing resources for the growth and development of these important collections. The language holdings vary from branch to branch and reflect current settlement patterns. The program has provided a solid foundation for introducing language, stories, and the library to newcomer families.

LEAP: A Comprehensive and Multifaceted After-School Program

Sandra Anne Farrell and Sandra Miller
Free Library of Philadelphia
Philadelphia, Pennsylvania

LEAP IS A FREE AFTER-SCHOOL PROGRAM offered at all 53 sites of the Free Library of Philadelphia. The program provides homework help, technology access and assistance, multicultural enrichment programs, technology workshops, and mentoring for children and teens.

LEAP began in 1989 as a privately funded pilot project for first to sixth graders and expanded over the years with support from the William Penn Foundation, PEW Charitable Trust, and other funders. In 1999, Mayor John Street recognized LEAP as a model after-school program and allocated city funds for it. In 2001, the city of Philadelphia assumed full funding of the LEAP program in every library and for grades 1–12 as part of the Free Library's general services operation budget.

Employment with a focus on positive youth development is an essential part of LEAP's success. The program employs 53 after-school leaders (college graduates) and 250 teen leadership assistants (high school students) to help the adult and children's librarians. When a teen leadership assistant graduates and enrolls at a local college, he or she is eligible to become an associate leader to provide mentoring for teen employees, technology and programming support, and a library speaker team. The associate leader program is a good recruitment tool for the library.

Training is another component of LEAP's success. All staff members are thoroughly trained in customer service, programming, positive youth development, homework help, technology, library resources, and effective library service. Elective workshops range from life skills training to SAT preparation, resume writing, and newsletter production. Each year, teen leadership assistants plan and participate in a daylong Youth Empowerment Summit at the Central Library for some 325 high school students from across the city.

LEAP incorporates national best practices in homework help, computer assistance, and positive youth development. It integrates library skills and information literacy into enjoyable learning experiences. Program participants proudly show librarians report cards with improving grades. Several teens said they never considered college until they became teen leadership assistants.

LEAP is recognized as a model by schools, families, elected officials, and youth organizations. The library partners with other city departments, administering, for example, a teen employment program for the Recreation Department. Community partners include the United Way, Philadelphia Safe and Sound (a nonprofit organization that works to improve the health and well-being of the city's youth), local colleges, the School District of Philadelphia, the Workforce Investment Board, and agencies in every neighborhood.

LEAP is a success because it meets the needs of the community by providing a quality program for young people in a safe, welcoming environment. It also benefits the library by providing much-needed staff during after-school hours. The program is important not only for the service it provides, but also for the role it plays in youth development. For participants, teen leadership assistants, and associate leaders, LEAP is more than an after-school program or job; it is an investment in the future of youth, communities, and the city of Philadelphia.

Libraries as Community Builders: The Greensboro Experience

Steve Sumerford
Greensboro Public Library
Greensboro, North Carolina

LIBRARIANS OFTEN COMPLAIN THAT PEOPLE don't realize how much the library can do for their communities. In meetings at the local, state, and national level, I have often heard librarians say that they resent the fact that they are not "invited to the table" when community leaders develop committees and projects to tackle critical issues. That was our library's situation in Greensboro, North Carolina, until 1989, when an innovative assistant director named Sandy Neerman decided that we shouldn't wait to be invited to the table. "We should set the table ourselves," she said.

It was in this context that Neerman and other Greensboro Public Library staff decided that the library should be more involved in literacy work. They recognized that the most progressive approach to literacy work was learner-centered, community-based, and holistic, and that more than just remedial classes and tutoring are necessary to increase a community's literacy levels. The library created literacy programs based on the recognition that the person being tutored also lives in a family, a neighborhood, and a city. The library sought to supplement its literacy-rich environment with initiatives sponsored by other community institutions.

After researching the community and meeting one on one with community leaders, the library staff initiated two strategies:

The first strategy was to *bring all of the key literacy providers and stakeholders to the table*. The library created a coalition of more than 20 organizations with a simple mission of promoting reading and literacy. This was an example of "setting the table" ourselves, rather than waiting to be invited to the table. The goal of the coalition, called the Community of Readers, was to bring together all agencies that had an interest in improving literacy skills. Employers, social service agencies, media, and others joined the effort. Many of the coalition's recommendations and partnerships have come to fruition. The community college and the library now cosponsor five classes per week at the library. The YWCA, the school system, and the library developed a family literacy program that serves teen parents.

The second strategy was to *improve the library's own literacy resources and programs*. The library transformed a branch library that was located in a low-income section of the city into an active lifelong learning center. The Vance Chavis Lifelong Learning Library became the hub of literacy services and has received numerous awards and grants for its innovative literacy programs. The success of this branch influenced the development of service strategies for a new branch library in a neighborhood populated with refugees and immigrants from more than 10 countries. Again, the library convened a meeting of service providers and neighborhood residents. We determined that we needed a nontraditional library—one that was devoted to teaching literacy skills to speakers of other languages and one that raised the city's awareness of the assets and needs of various ethnic groups. The Glenwood Library opened in 1996, featuring a comprehensive English as a second language program. About three hundred adults come each week to improve their English skills using computer labs, tutors, small-group instruction, and special classes. Many immigrants visit the Glenwood Library during their first month in the city, and it is not uncommon to hear them say, "Glenwood is my second home."

When the Lila Wallace-Reader's Digest Fund sought proposals from libraries around the nation for its literacy initiative, the Greensboro Public Library demonstrated that it had a strong track record of library-based literacy instruction, local funding, and community partnerships. On the strength of that record, the library was awarded $400,000 from the fund.

This work demonstrates that a strong outreach program can meet the needs of library users while raising the profile of the library system and changing its image in the city. The Greensboro Public Library now has a stronger image as a community problem solver and community builder. It is called upon to participate in numerous high-level community projects. This would not have happened if we had not had:

- innovative leadership at the top of the organization
- programs that were based on the needs of the community
- willingness to provide leadership to a community-based coalition
- continuous funding from the library and other funders
- a nontraditional staff that fit the mission of these two branches
- a strategic plan for the library that reflected its role as a community problem solver

TIP Service: Community Information and Referral @Your Library

Margaret Gillis Bruni
Detroit Public Library
Detroit, Michigan

DESPITE SOME ENCOURAGING RECENT ECONOMIC developments and improving social indicators, Detroit remains a troubled city. An estimated 22 percent of households fall beneath the federal poverty level, while 47 percent of adults are considered functionally illiterate.

The situation was just as bleak in 1973, when Clara Stanton Jones, then director of the Detroit Public Library, committed the library to helping disadvantaged residents resolve the problems they faced every day. At that time, many Detroiters would not think to turn to a library for help in finding things like bus schedule information, repair manuals for older cars, or low-cost ideas for preparing nutritious meals. Many residents were also in the dark about the spectrum of community services that were available to help them improve their quality of life—things like emergency groceries, health clinics, and job training programs.

Jones envisioned the Detroit Public Library as a central access point for practical information of all sorts, and she realized that the residents who were most in need of this information were not traditional library users. She faced two challenges. The first was to make Detroiters understand that the library was *relevant* to them, and the second was to make the library more *accessible* to a traditionally disenfranchised group.

Her solution was to launch the TIP Service, a single phone number that people could call for help with anything.

- Need to know the name of the fourth vice president of the United States? Call TIP.
- Looking for groceries until food stamps arrive next week? Call TIP for a referral to a food pantry.
- Can't find a recipe for gingerbread? TIP can help.
- Don't know who to complain to about a contractor who won't finish the job he began at your home? TIP can tell you what to do.

Today, TIP is the oldest and most widely known community information program operating out of an American public library. More than 15,000 calls come into the TIP service line at the Main Library each year, augmented by an ever-rising number of e-mail requests.

Four factors contribute to TIP's success:

1. The Detroit Public Library never made a distinction between community information and referral requests and more traditional library reference questions. The library could help with anything. This simple marketing message resonated with people who were not accustomed to using reference services or who viewed the library only as a support for educational or recreational needs.
2. From the start, TIP was integrated into the library's operations and culture. While TIP staff had to develop new resources and skills (e.g., how to catalog community programs as well as monographs), the message was communicated to all staff that TIP librarians do what librarians have always done: collect and catalog information, conduct reference interviews, and provide information. Other community information programs fail when library staff perceive them as social work programs that are peripheral or even antithetical to the institution's mission.
3. Library administration supported TIP staff in their efforts to develop working relationships with local, state, and national human services organizations. These collaborations helped to keep TIP focused on its community mission and raised the library's profile in the community, particularly among governmental and nonprofit agencies.
4. TIP capitalized on the library's unique role in the organization of information to develop a comprehensive database of community resources. The database's utility to other organizations in the community solidified

the library's position as a local leader in the information field and helped secure funds to support the TIP operation.

TIP achieved the objectives of making the library accessible and relevant. By connecting to a single, widely publicized phone number, callers generally get the information they need or are referred to a resource that can help them resolve their problem. Thirty years after Clara Jones's initial vision, TIP continues to help the Detroit Public Library fulfill the original vision for the program.

Community Youth Corps: Teens as Library Resources

Deborah D. Taylor
Enoch Pratt Free Library
Baltimore, Maryland

A MULTIYEAR GRANT FROM THE WALLACE-Reader's Digest Funds served as the catalyst to reenergize young adult services at the Enoch Pratt Free Library in Baltimore. In partnership with the Baltimore Public Schools, the Pratt Library developed a program called Community Youth Corps (CYC). This highly successful program has benefited both program participants and the library's staff.

Teens in Baltimore schools are required to complete 75 hours of community service for high school graduation. The library is an approved site to earn those credits. Teens who participate in the Community Youth Corps are not paid, but they receive high-quality work experiences, training opportunities, and exposure to the library's vast resources.

The structure of the Community Youth Corps evolved from focus groups and surveys of teens, their parents or caregivers, and professionals who work with teens. Teens were especially interested in having opportunities to earn service learning credit while developing their own skills. Young adults typically enter the program in eighth grade and participate through the tenth grade. Employment opportunities in branches and the Central Library are available at the end of the program.

Following are some of the successful outcomes of the Community Youth Corps.

More teens use the library as a resource. Teens who participate in CYC learn about the library's many resources as they work. We encourage them to refer friends and classmates to the program and to the library. Since the inception of the CYC, the number of teens attending programs and using the library has increased. The opportunity to gain service learning hours has been attractive to teens who may not have seen the library as a place to spend time.

Teens plan and coordinate library programs for peers. It is critical to hear from teens about programs and activities they want in their libraries. Program planning involves interviews and focus groups with teens, parents, youth workers, and library staff. Programs are developed on the basis of the information gathered at those sessions. A recent survey of CYC participants and other teens led to successful programs on personal safety, anime production, painting and drawing, and financial aid for college.

Teens are trained to develop technology, employment, and leadership skills. Training received in the Community Youth Corps can translate into meaningful job skills. The training covers library skills, customer service, computer technology, and video production. Teens are able to assist with the summer reading programs and computer classes for patrons. They also produce public service announcements for library programs. All training sessions are conducted by trainers who are skilled in working with young adults.

Teens have an understanding of career opportunities in libraries. Shadowing of library staff gives CYC participants firsthand knowledge of the duties performed by librarians and other library staff. They are exposed to the variety of skills needed to provide information and library resources to customers. Teens who complete the program understand how to prepare for a future in librarianship and related fields.

Staff has a greater appreciation of teens as customers and workers at the library. The Community Youth Corps has invigorated the library's services to young adults and expanded its capacity to involve hard-to-reach young adults in its programs. CYC participants are viewed as resources and on-site advisers for library staff to consult about young adult services and programs and the best ways to interest and reach their peers.

After the grant funding ended, the Enoch Pratt Library incorporated the program into its ongoing service plan. Other community partners have recognized the value of the Community Youth Corps model. For example, a new after-school initiative, the Safe and Sound Campaign for the Improvement of Services for Children, Youth and Family, will place teens who are interested in computer technology in the library's CYC program in the summer months. The same project is seeking to train teen storytellers to perform at libraries and other venues in the community. The library also serves as a designated site for Youth Works, Baltimore's summer job program for teen workers.

Global Outreach Services: Outreach in Academic Libraries

Thelma H. Tate
Rutgers University
New Brunswick, New Jersey

THE GLOBAL OUTREACH PROGRAM WAS ESTABLISHED at Rutgers University in 1999 to extend library services to local, regional, national, and international levels. The program seeks to increase and diversify the university libraries' target audiences; to implement innovative programs and services; and to strengthen the libraries' institutional partnerships. Global outreach supports the university libraries' long-range plan for more active contribution to campus and civic life.

The many activities of the program led to a greater understanding of world cultures, highlighted the information and literacy needs in developing countries, and empowered people to contribute resources that make a difference. Many of these initiatives have been incorporated into ongoing partnerships that extend from our local libraries to communities around the world. Following are some examples of successful program activities.

We held seminars to let staff, students, faculty, and our surrounding communities know how they could contribute to information and literacy projects. For example, Rutgers library staff was instrumental in launching the Global Literacy Project (www.glpinc.org) in 2000, with the goal of fostering public education programs in the United States and abroad. Since its inception, the project has shipped out more than 300,000 volumes of books and journals and established several multimedia learning centers.

We highlighted the cultural diversity among our staff, faculty, and students through formal and informal programs in the libraries. For example, a few library staff members conducted a seminar on Chinese art and culture, in which they detailed their experiences as participants in an art class led by a Chinese painter. They explained how they gained a greater knowledge of Chinese culture by exploring its artistic traditions. They compared their experience to that of a new library user who at first is unsure about how to get started on a project or how to ask the right questions but then is filled with excitement when he or she masters the research techniques needed to complete a project. They noted a new understanding of how to help these first-time users.

In 2001, we established the Rutgers Internship Program for African Archivists and Manuscript Curators to address problems of preservation and access to archival materials in national and university archives of Tanzania. The program was developed in association with Columbia University, New York University, the Schomburg Center for Research in Black Culture, and the U.S. National Archives (North East Region). The intern gained theoretical knowledge and practical experience that he used to improve Tanzania's methods for collecting, organizing, preserving, and making documents available to policy makers, scholars, and citizens worldwide.

The outreach activities described here have improved communication and work relations in the Rutgers libraries. Library staff and faculty members who were formerly mere acquaintances now enjoy regular conversations. These relationships encourage faculty to tap into the staff's expertise and to feel comfortable using the different parts of the library system. This sense of collegiality and ownership has enhanced library services at the university.

PART 3

Outreach Using Information Technology

Kathleen (KG) Ouye
San Mateo Public Library
San Mateo, California

■ OUTREACH OFTEN INVOLVES COURTING NEW customers who may have encountered barriers to the full range of information services at our libraries. We often do not understand the depth of those barriers. How many times have librarians said, "if only people knew what we had to offer"? Technology has been a lifesaver as we attempt to lure and connect people to the useful resources that enable libraries to change lives. The provision of free and reliable access to the Internet was a simple but revolutionary "aha!" moment for the library profession and for those we serve.

Of course, it is really not that simple. A young immigrant mother wonders if there will be computer access in the small, temporary site in her neighborhood. She expresses the need for access at her local library even though more than half of American families have computer access in their homes or offices. This is because libraries provide service users do not have at home or office:

- Libraries support users who may have language or literacy barriers.
- Libraries support users who may not have the skills to use all the information services we offer. (Think about those databases!)
- Libraries provide access to up-to-date equipment in working order.
- Libraries make access more efficient via high-speed networks.

It is the assistance with navigating the vast sea of information that makes libraries and librarians so valuable.

For all the accompanying procedural headaches, e-rate and state-matching funds have poured millions of dollars into libraries to support their technological infrastructures. This legislation is an acknowledgment of the role that libraries play in their respective communities. Libraries are essential in the provision of resources to the public—in online formats as well as in books, magazines, newspapers, etc. Such access to information is the basis of a vibrant and informed society.

We still face funding challenges, but we also face new challenges of changing infrastructures, development of staff and user skills, and finding relevant and appropriate content. Our role as information providers requires that libraries meet those challenges and resolve the problems that user demands have brought to our attention. If this seems daunting, look at it as a twenty-first century WPA project—as we work to create new tools and platforms for our users, we ensure our continued employment. The public's expectation of improved access and content enables us to operate from a position of strength as we approach our governing and funding sources.

The models that follow demonstrate creativity in the face of adversity. It's as if the lack of funding or tough circumstances brings out the best ideas for using technology to solve long-standing problems. The models demonstrate many types of partnerships and collaborations—with other libraries, government agencies, nonprofits, and private sector organizations. An environment with fewer resources is an impetus to seek partnerships outside traditional spheres, while an abundance of resources seems to keep our creativity within our respective silos. Outreach is invaluable to our users and to us, the service providers.

Major national and regional telecommunications companies have assessed the current state of technology deployment and the challenges of the future. Most industry leaders now acknowledge the role libraries play in providing access to technology and in developing relevant content. They also acknowledge the challenges of that role. Advanced communications can promote economic growth, jobs, education, and social benefits. There are industries flourishing now that did not exist a generation ago. But the warnings from those industries echo the library profession's own fears: information technology can disrupt the status quo.

Look at the following models and ask yourself:

> Can some part of the model be applied to a local problem?
>
> Are your clients facing similar problems?
>
> Who are your potential partners?
>
> Can you be a champion of the model?

Then step back and ask broader questions about your library that can help you build new models:

> What are our core skills?
>
> What can we bring to the table that adds value for everyone?
>
> How can we create new customers or improve service to current ones?
>
> Who are potential creative partners?

With all technology models, the human factor is the key. Chasing money can be a great motivator, but the funding has to address a need. A commitment to service is the key to sustaining an outreach model. Technology is a conduit for that commitment.

Central Valley Digital Network: Partners in Bridging the Digital Divide

Carol Whiteside
Great Valley Center
Modesto, California

GREAT VALLEY CENTER (WWW.GREATVALLEY .org) is a nonprofit organization that supports the economic, social, and environmental well-being of California's Central Valley. The valley is a vast agricultural region, one of the fastest growing and poorest in the nation. Analysis conducted by the center confirmed that the digital divide was greater here than in the rest of the state. Many immigrants, poor people, and rural families did not have access to computers or the skills to use them.

The Central Valley Digital Network was created to help rural residents get connected to technology and to provide services and training to people in traditionally unserved and underserved communities. Several libraries in California's Central Valley have joined a larger network of agencies to achieve those goals.

In four years, Central Valley Digital Network has placed 25 AmeriCorps *VISTA (Volunteers in Service to America) personnel at 31 sites in 11 counties of the Central Valley. Nonprofit organizations, libraries in particular, were invited to apply for volunteer placements. Libraries were selected on the basis of their willingness and ability to host a volunteer (e.g., to provide work space and to supervise his or her work), their interest in technology, the level of service currently in place, and their willingness to send supervisors to training.

To ensure a successful project year, the Central Valley Digital Network supports its VISTA personnel and partner sites in many ways.

- The network conducts VISTA training seminars on community outreach, volunteer management, technology skill development, media outreach, public speaking, and other topics.

- The network's Innovation Fund gives VISTAs a chance to apply for small grants to design innovative projects that support technology services at their sites and within their communities.

- The network offers competitive scholarships to VISTAs who wish to learn additional software, office productivity, or computer troubleshooting skills.

- The network sends its VISTAs to technology conferences around the country—past conferences have been in San Diego, San Francisco, and Washington, D.C.

- The network builds esprit de corps among VISTAs throughout the Central Valley through recreational trips, group activities, meetings, and resource sharing.

In their years of service, VISTA staff members have set up many ongoing programs and services. They have conducted technology literacy training, developed multilingual training materials, launched public outreach campaigns, organized technology-related projects that respond to the community's unique needs, built community partnerships, and recruited and trained volunteers and staff to teach others about technology.

Following are just a few examples of how partnerships with the Central Valley Digital Network have enhanced the delivery of technology-related services in library settings.

The Stanislaus County Library hosts Bridges to Technology, a program that offers free technology workshops at all 13 branches in the county. VISTA staff created a system for recruiting, training, and scheduling local volunteers to lead the workshops. They also developed a curriculum in English and Spanish. More than 40 volunteers have joined the program. Workshop topics include computer basics, beginning Internet, intermediate Internet, Microsoft Word 2000, genealogy research on the Web, and making cards in PrintShop (www.stanislauslibrary.org/involvebridg.shtml).

For some time the Lodi Public Library was not equipped to support substantive technology training for its users: the library's computer center was open 20 hours a week, with only 5 volunteer trainers. The partnership with Central Valley Digital Network helped open the computer learning center, which is open 53 hours a week, has 25 committed volunteers, and offers multilingual training for our diverse users—28 percent Hispanic, 22 percent seniors, and 7 percent Indian/Punjabi. A grant award enabled the purchase of a new computer and an assistive technology device called QuadJoy, which allows a user to operate the computer with his mouth. Another project trains high-school seniors to use software to create short videos. In the last three months of 2003, the center recorded 2,649 user sessions—the same number recorded for the entire year before the partnership with Central Valley Digital Network (www.lodi.gov/library/).

The Sutter County Library had just completed an upgrade of 18 new public access computer workstations, including one Spanish language workstation. Although public interest was high, library staff noticed that many of the users needed basic computer skills. Staff from the Central Valley Digital Network supplemented the library's computer classes for seniors with small-group and one-on-one instruction. They also offered small group instruction in Spanish serving about 20 residents per week. Network volunteers helped to set up computers at four branches, bringing Internet access to outlying areas of the county (www.co.sutter.ca.us/index.aspx?doc=/depts/ library/library.xml).

The Yuba County Library increased awareness and availability of technology resources at the library through its partnership with the Central Valley Digital Network. Community members, including the 60 percent to 70 percent senior population the library serves, learned to navigate the Internet and use e-mail. Classes at the library were promoted through networking and outreach to local media. Volunteers were recruited to translate computer workshop materials for Spanish speakers (www.co.yuba.ca.us/library/library).

Overall, volunteers from the Central Valley Digital Network have presented 20,484 user training sessions at community technology centers, libraries, government agencies, and nonprofit organizations throughout the Central Valley. The organization believes that access to technology must be accompanied by access to content that is of value and interest to the user, and by the ability to find and evaluate the information. Libraries are effective partners in providing such access.

www.firstfind.info: Organizing Easy-to-Use Information on the Web

Robin Osborne
Westchester Library System
Ardsley, New York

SEVERAL LIBRARY SYSTEMS IN THE NEW YORK metropolitan area provide services to a large and diverse population. Although the Brooklyn Public Library, New York Public Library, Queens Borough Public Library, and Westchester Library System are officially distinct institutions, staff and administrators share common concerns and practices that support improved services to new Americans, low-level readers, and other users with special information needs. We are especially aware of how the increase in immigrant populations in the region has dramatically affected the demand for information in plain language that helps local residents navigate the spheres of work and family.

We have always shared information on acquiring books, pamphlets, videos, and other materials that provide information at various levels of comprehension. We realized, however, that we have been remiss in transferring that skill range to the technological resources that we proudly feature in our promotional materials and annual reports. The ability to find, comprehend, and use information in the on-line chaos known as the Internet can be daunting to those who are not seasoned computer users, are not fluent in the taglines and shortcuts used by Web publishers, or do not know how to evaluate or validate the content of a website.

Administrators and outreach staff from the four systems discussed ways to share staff expertise to develop resources that could be used at any point of access. We submitted a successful Library Services and Technology Act proposal to build a virtual library that could provide information access for target constituencies that we all serve. We invited the ALA's Office for Literacy and Outreach Services to participate to create a national forum about the project for other libraries.

And so www.firstfind.info was born.[1] More than 40 staff members from the four systems have contributed to the collection of more than 900 websites that cover 14 topics, including education, families, jobs, and health. It has gained recognition as a unique resource on the Web. The site received an award of distinction from the National Institute for Literacy. Many national and international agencies link to firstfind.info, including The Children's Partnership, UNESCO, the Harvard School of Public Health, and the National Adult Literacy Database of Canada.

The firstfind.info website is now an ongoing project of the Westchester Library System's outreach services department. The staff is exploring partnerships with community groups to promote use of the site and contributions to enhance its content. One project with a local prenatal clinic will support a small computer lab at the clinic, with volunteer technical assistants to help clients find health information via firstfind.info. Staff at the health education graduate program at Sarah Lawrence College submitted a grant proposal to create text about specific health issues to post on firstfind.info.

Firstfind.info is a valuable resource for librarians and end users, regardless of geographic or institutional boundaries. It offers opportunities for further collaboration as we seek to expand the collection of resources. We will continue to offer workshops on how to identify information needs and evaluate content for the widest net of library users at national and regional library conferences.

Librarians can play a vital role in making the Web a true information highway if we affirm our professional responsibility to deliver equitable information services via universally accessible content.

NOTE

1. Firstfind.info, "Easy to Find, Easy to Use Websites in Plain and Simple English," a pamphlet about the development of the project. Available at www.ala.org/Content/ NavigationMenu/Our_Association/Offices/Literacy_and_Outreach_Services/ Outreach_Resources/firstfind_compilation.pdf. Accessed 16 January 2004.

Indigenous Peoples and Information Technology

Loreine Roy and Antony Cherian
School of Information
University of Texas at Austin

INDIAN COUNTRY IS HOME TO CHALLENGES and innovations in information technology. Challenges are seen in providing access to even basic technologies. According to a 1995 U.S. census survey, 53 percent of Native homes do not have a telephone. On the Pine Ridge Reservation, 39 percent of the homes lack electricity, and many do not have indoor plumbing.

In 1995, the U.S. Congress issued a report on telecommunications in Indian country. It stated, "Absent some kind of policy interventions, Native Americans are unlikely to catch up with and probably will fall further behind, the majority society with respect to telecommunications."[1]

Yet indigenous communities in the United States are using information technology in a variety of efforts. Key among these is Native language revitalization. The health of its language may be the greatest indicator of the well-being of an indigenous culture. Once, between three hundred and six hundred indigenous languages were spoken in North America. Now, only 211 languages are spoken and only 32 of these are spoken by people of all ages.

Much attention is being given to Native language revitalization, due in large part to the passage of the Native American Languages Act of 1990. The act declares, "It is the policy of the United States to preserve, protect, and promote the rights and freedom of Native Americans to use, practice, and develop Native American languages."

Information technology can support language recovery because it reaches many people in a variety of formats. The University of Alaska provided a for-credit distance learning class on Deg Xinang, the Ingalik Athabaskan language spoken in central Alaska. Native speakers conversed with one or two students by telephone for an hour each week. Radio station KTNN has served as the Voice of the Navajo Nation since 1986, providing programming in Navajo that includes the morning livestock report, local and regional news, weather, and the Navajo Word of the Day. The Intertribal Wordpath Society of Oklahoma produces *Wordpath*, a weekly half-hour television show on Indian languages of the state.

The University of Hawaii at Manoa has used electronic discussion lists, the Hawaii Interactive Television System, and collaborative writing software (Daedalus) for communication and content delivery. Students and faculty have also used multimedia to author websites to support Hawaiian language study. Other key organizations and events for language recovery include the Indigenous Language Institute (New Mexico), the annual American Indian Language Development Institute (Arizona), and the Sovereign Nations Preservation Project (Texas).

Tribal community libraries are becoming important partners in language recovery efforts. A Tewa language study group meets in the Santa Clara (New Mexico) Pueblo Community Library. Elders of the Pala Band of Mission Indians in California are available in the library to offer Cupeno language tutoring and to assist in developing Native language curriculum. The tribal community library serving the Wiyot (California) tribe developed a living language website. Other libraries develop and house language collections, including unique oral history materials.

Will technology support tribal sovereignty or contribute to the erosion of Native culture? Craig Howe, an Oglala Sioux, defines tribal sovereignty as consisting of four aspects:

- spatial (geographical or connection to the land)
- social (personal identity)
- spiritual (morality and ethics)
- experiential (ceremony and observance)

Technology alone will not enable a person to lead an indigenous life, but it can be a powerful tool if paired with cultural respect, tribal community ownership, and thoughtful community-centered discussion.

NOTE

1. Olga Kharif, "Native Americans Stake a High-Tech Claim." Available at www .businessweek.com/bwdaily/dnflash/nov2001/nf2011126_0470.htm. Accessed 15 January 2004.

Outreach Efforts at the Hope Fox Eccles Clinical Library

Liz Workman
Hope Fox Eccles Clinical Library
University of Utah
Salt Lake City, Utah

THE HOPE FOX ECCLES CLINICAL LIBRARY IS a branch of the Spencer S. Eccles Health Sciences Library and is located in University Hospital on the University of Utah campus at Salt Lake City. In addition to serving clinician and consumer patrons within University Hospital, clinical library staff members have developed technological tools to extend health information to individuals far beyond its boundaries. These tools include the Utah Consumer Health Information Network and the 24 Languages Project.

THE UTAH CONSUMER HEALTH INFORMATION NETWORK

The Utah Consumer Health Information Network (UCHIN) supplies information on local health services for Utah residents and provides access to preevaluated health information sources.

In late 1999, members of the Utah Library Association noted the need for an on-line resource that addressed residents' need to locate services and quality health information on-line. The Utah Library Association partnered with the Hope Fox Eccles Clinical Library and its parent organization, the Spencer S. Eccles Health Sciences Library, to establish the UCHIN network. Its website, http://uchin.med.utah.edu, guides users to reliable consumer health information sources though layperson-oriented categories. These categories include sections on health and wellness, diseases and conditions, and the unique health needs of specific audiences. The Locating Resources section connects users to hospitals, providers, libraries facilitating health research, and many other regional health-oriented services. Under Organizations, for example, users can find local contact information and more for services as diverse as emergency food assistance and help for senior citizens.

UCHIN recently partnered with the Pioneer Project (http://pioneer-library.org), a statewide network of academic, school, and public libraries. The Pioneer Project sponsors an on-line library of electronic resources for Utah residents. UCHIN is the premier health information provider of Pioneer's public library component, which is accessible from any computer connected to the Internet. This partnership enables a larger audience to access free consumer health information.

The UCHIN partnership also includes the Utah Health Sciences Library Consortium. Hospital and corporate libraries from throughout Utah work together within this consortium to improve services for their patrons. Consortium members contribute to the development of the UCHIN site and help to expand the project's resources. Hope Fox Eccles Clinical Library staff members maintain the current website.

THE 24 LANGUAGES PROJECT

The 24 Languages Project provides free access to more than two hundred non-English consumer-oriented health publications through its website, http://medstat.med.utah.edu/24languages.

The project began as a collaborative effort of the library and the Utah Department of Health's Bureau of Primary Care, Rural and Ethnic Health. The bureau contributed hard copies of multilingual brochures addressing consumer health issues. Clinical Library staff scanned the printed materials to create digital pdf representations and developed a website that serves as an access point to the multilingual pdf brochures. A Library Services and Technology Act grant funded this work.

The 24 Languages Project website contains materials from several partner organizations and agencies, including the Association of Asian Pacific Community Health Organizations, the Immunization Action Coalition, and the federal government. These partner organizations translate a wide range of consumer health information into non-English languages as part of their effort to improve the health of many diverse populations. Partner organizations contribute the translated documents, which are either scanned and uploaded to the project's server or accessed directly via link to another website. Languages range from Arabic to Vietnamese, and the brochures are organized by language. The website also provides access to other similar on-line resources.

The National Network of Libraries of Medicine recently awarded funding to the 24 Languages Project to create on-line sound recordings—an important tool for people with low literacy skills or visual impairments. Project staff work with individuals and groups on and off the university campus to locate native speakers of various languages to record 200 on-line brochures. After the brochures are recorded, the project technician posts them to the website for downloading or streaming. Project staff market the recordings through partnerships with community groups, workshops at regional professional conferences, and "train the trainer" workshops at libraries and other facilities throughout the state. Regional media serving the area's diverse cultures also advertise this service.

Web usage statistics indicate a positive response to both of these projects from the on-line community. The Hope Fox Eccles Clinical Library staff is pleased with the results and enthusiastic about potential outreach possibilities that future technologies might provide.

Info Seekers and the Biotech Learning Center: Building for the Future

Jean O. Crispieri
San Mateo Pubic Library
San Mateo, California

THE CITY OF SAN MATEO NEEDS A NEW LIBRARY building, and this need has fostered two exciting projects that will offer innovative information services for a wide range of students, based on unique facilities design and a long-term community commitment to provide funds to build services and bridge the information technology gap.

The San Mateo Public Library will open the doors to its new building in summer 2006. As the library sought support to build the new facility with a local bond issue and private donations, we became aware of another opportunity for a matching grant from the state, which required a joint program with local schools. The library and the local school district discussed the opportunity and agreed to collaborate on a program. City council members, the school board, appointed officials, and staff were invited to contribute to the discussion.

The collaboration led to the development of Info Seekers, an educational program targeted to fourth- and fifth-grade students. The objective of the program is to teach students how to use the modern library to find, evaluate, and integrate information to create a report, multimedia project, or other student work. This training in library skills will be a required part of the school curriculum.

Info Seekers will occupy a dedicated space in the new library and will be equipped with specially configured workstations adjacent to the main Information Services Center. Students will be taken to the public library to fulfill their assignments. Teachers, school and library staff, and trained volunteers will be on site to guide students to the print and electronic resources they need to complete their assignments. Library and school staffs are planning the services and training that will be needed to use the 850-square-foot help center and its eight computer workstations.

As Info Seekers took shape, the library wanted to extend this model to create another unique learning environment for high school and college students in the new building. This model would be developed as a biotechnology/life sciences learning center. Because San Mateo is at the geographic center of the worldwide biotechnology industry, developing skilled workers for the regional industry is critical to retain the industry leadership role that supports the economic health of the San Francisco Bay Area. The library's Biotech Learning Center will promote education and interest in life sciences and prepare students for careers in the biotech industry.

Built around an innovative presentation of the library's life sciences collection, the Biotech Learning Center will bring together flexible study and meeting spaces; high-speed technology; teaching equipment; workstations; and electronic resources on health, nutrition, and science. The center will be physically linked with Info Seekers. Between the two learning areas is a glass-walled seminar room that can accommodate up to 40 people in a classroom configuration. The seminar space can convert to a group study room and meeting area.

The models of Info Seekers and the Biotech Learning Center will be expanded to serve nonstudent users as well. Because biotechnology and health sciences play an increasingly important role in the life of any library user, a dedicated librarian will be appointed to provide ongoing assistance. The librarian's work will be funded through an endowment created by donations from biotechnology companies and individual investors. Physician volunteers will also help library users to access information, to interpret it, and to frame questions to ask their health care providers. The new library building will welcome all visitors to explore the life sciences and other disciplines that many people now find inaccessible.

With Info Seekers and the Biotech Learning Center, San Mateo is giving the community a chance to develop skills and access information in ways that foster discovery, creativity, and, ultimately, success. Our new library building will be a community center that sustains learning for the future.

PART 4

Technical Services: Connecting Minds

Zora J. Sampson
University of Wisconsin–Barron County
Rice Lake, Wisconsin

LIBRARIES ARE SYSTEMS THAT ACCURATELY organize, access, and preserve all human knowledge. The most important thing librarians do in this system is connect minds. To make these connections, we have to embrace a communication model that supports clear and continuous dialogue among three minds:

- the minds encapsulated in the materials we collect or of the living resources we call upon
- the mind of the user (present or at a distance)
- the mind of the librarian

FLOW OF INFORMATION

As librarians, we connect a user (physically or virtually) to the resources we offer. The mind of the librarian, active and informed, is intrinsic to the success of this connection. The minds of those who contribute to our collections receive added value from technical services librarians, who make materials more accessible through local cataloging, preservation, labeling, and other processes.

As we seek to increase modes of access, alter physical arrangement, or revise collection policies to improve services to our users, we must do so with caution. All our efforts affect the ability of our users to connect with the information they need. If we want them to stay connected, we must make them feel comfortable about requesting assistance and alerting library staff to their accessing difficulties. User feedback is a good tool for assessing a library's technical services.

COMMUNICATING LOCALLY

Librarians provide equitable delivery of services by enabling the flow of information among the three minds noted earlier. We must act locally to enhance the usability of our resources for children, senior citizens, people with disabilities, and other underserved users. Our commitment to serving the broadest possible user base must be built into the structure of *each* service, *each* choice of subject headings that are relevant and culturally aware, *each* selection process, *each* evaluation of systems and services, *each* informed purchase of materials and technology, and *each* rearrangement and presentation of resources.

We've learned that on-line databases of full-text journal articles are convenient for storage and index access, although they may come at the loss of local control. If we lose access to journal titles that have no on-site print counterparts, it is due to failed contract negotiations with vendors rather than thoughtful weeding.

Does your library seek the input of technical services staff and users in selecting electronic and other services? As information scientists, technical services librarians can make valuable contributions in negotiating access to resources, such as requiring contracts for interlibrary loan requests for electronic journals to be fulfilled in print or electronically. That is outreach in technical services.

COLLECTION MAINTENANCE AND ACCESS

We must keep sight of the three minds in our communication model as we address collection maintenance or we will unconsciously restrict user access. Multilingual collections, like all service delivery areas, present new challenges and opportunities in collection development and cataloging that attract and satisfy diverse interests, ages, and abilities. We need to be sure that our collections reflect the particular interests of each group, as well as being comprehensive in core resources essential to all groups.

And let's not forget maintenance of our physical collections. The repair of books is more important than you may realize—more is lost than the pages when books fall apart. I used to volunteer to teach English for the Laubach Literacy program. I heard my student chastise her child for bringing home a library book in disrepair. She was afraid that she would be fined for the condition of the book, something the family could not afford. She told her daughter to never again bring home a book so old and worn. I could not help but understand the concern, and felt that the library had let this family down. We need to learn about how our services are perceived in the mind of this mother and all users.

Technical services staff expertly broaden access to rare and fragile collections of books and other media. Digitization of materials to which access was formerly limited due to preservation concerns is significantly increasing public awareness and access. Digitization offers broader availability to federal, state, and local government documents that can assist communities in planning and mapping. How we organize and make those materials available could comprise an entire study in outreach models. Even as we laud these initiatives, we must also advocate for funding that provides hardware, software, and instructional resources to ensure their availability to the widest range of potential users.

With new ways of organizing, accessing, and storing recorded minds in more formats than ever, we must deal with new cataloging languages. From MARC to metadata, from html to xml, whatever the next advent, librarians bear a responsibility to direct these advances in communication technology and ensure that they facilitate connections between the minds of users and materials. We must sharpen our own vision and skills to create dynamic infrastructures, finding aids, and other tools that facilitate information retrieval for diverse users.

As we move to more on-line delivery, we must strive for barrier-free presentation. Even physical aids such as wheelchairs and alternative interface computers are wasted if they are not obviously placed in our buildings and promoted with signage. Funding for physical aids becomes harder to sustain if the devices are unused.

LIVING OUR COMMUNICATION MODEL

Technology enables communication to take place over shorter time, greater distance, and in mass quantity. As our users and their needs become more diverse and as technological advances expand service capabilities, technical services units bear a greater burden to perfect communication strategies. Whether we are adding reference access for distant learners or helping faculty and students connect through course management software and electronic reserves, we are reaching further every day.

Outreach toward diversity is not just a noble effort. It is essential for the health, growth, and endurance of our living system. Social psychologist Erich Jantsch observes that constant renewal is a characteristic of living systems.[1] If we want libraries to endure, we must strive not for stability, but for change, evolution, and adaptation—juggling chaos to maintain harmonious balance. If our communication model enables ongoing improvement of access, preservation, and storage, library systems will continue to nurture the growth of human knowledge for future generations.

NOTE

1. Erich Jantsch, *The Self-Organizing Universe: Scientific and Human Implications of the Emerging Paradigm of Evolution* (New York: Pergamon, 1980).

A Librarian's Librarian: Albert P. Marshall

Satia Marshall Orange
Office for Literacy and Outreach Services
American Library Association
Chicago, Illinois

I REMEMBER THREE-BY-FIVE CARDS, EVERY-where, all over my father's desk in the library, all over his desk at home, in shoeboxes, in his pockets, on bookshelves and windowsills—everywhere, really. He was always writing or typing notes about newspaper and magazine articles, speeches, books, interviews—everything. He had a special gift, which he considered a responsibility, to collect all kinds of information, to organize it, and to make it available to others. What use was information if it wasn't readily available?

My father was Albert P. Marshall. A book about him and his work, *The Marshall Index: A Guide to Negro Periodical Literature, 1940–1946,* was published by ProQuest Information and Learning Systems in 2002. The significance of this publication is stated by editor Richard Newman:

> . . . it made accessible for the first time the contents of the major African-American periodicals of the early 1940s. This was a critical period; it was between the time when freedom was in the air because of the ideology of World War II, and the smashing of legalized segregation by the Supreme Court's *Brown* decision of 1955.[1]

Initially, journals of African American scholarship were included, such as the *Journal of Negro History; Journal of Negro Education; Opportunity, the Journal of the National Urban League;* and journals and bulletins of some black colleges and universities. The list would grow to include *Ebony, Negro Digest, Monthly Summary of Events and Trends in Race Relations,* and other small publications. Newman continued:

> To create the index, Marshall adapted subject headings from the *Readers' Guide to Periodical Literature* and wrote citations on three-by-five cards, which he filed in a shoebox. He typed mimeograph stencils, ran off copies, and mailed the *Guide* (in an original edition of 100 copies) to a handful of subscribers. The yearly subscription rate was $2.70, with single copies of the first three quarterly issues for sale at 40 cents each. The fourth quarterly issue, which consisted of new entries cumulated with those of the first three issues, could be bought separately for $2. Purchasers of a year's subscription also received a loose-leaf notebook in which to file their copies. At the end of 1942, the second year of publication, Marshall announced there were more than 50 subscribers of the regular issues and an additional 50 for the cumulation alone.[2]

Publication of the indexes was interrupted by military service from 1942 to 1946. By then, a few of the magazines were included in general periodical indexes, but not all. The scholarly works of black colleges and universities were recognized within those communities but seldom outside them.

The impact of this work is its documentation of 41 titles that are seldom indexed anywhere else. For librarians, it demonstrates how the application of our professional skills to preserve and access these often obscure works published in local communities can open doors for future generations.

My father's career moved him to Lincoln University in Missouri and finally to Eastern Michigan University. He demonstrated leadership in state and national organizations, including ALA Council and Executive Board. He cherished his connections with his various communities even more, which resulted in many articles, books, and presentations, all formulated on those same three-by-five cards.

In his late seventies he became more dependent on the computer, although he still used the cards to develop his writings. He published transcriptions of oral histories and related researches of African Americans in early Ypsilanti, Michigan, many of whom were involved in the Underground Railroad. To ensure broader accessibility to these stories, especially for family members of the storytellers, *Unconquered Souls: The History of the African American in Ypsilanti* was published in large-print format.

My father died March 9, 2001, two weeks after e-mailing his last article to the *Ypsilanti Courier.* His work is not forgotten in that community, or by the rest of us. It's accessible through the Ypsilanti Historical Museum and in libraries across the state and nation for generations to come. And that was his purpose, after all.

NOTES

1. Richard Newman and James P. Danky, eds., *The Marshall Index: A Guide to Negro Periodical Literature, 1940–1946* (Ann Arbor, Mich.: ProQuest, 2002), ix.
2. Ibid., x.

Subject Access and Responsibility

Hope A. Olson
School of Information Studies
University of Wisconsin–Milwaukee

FOR DECADES WE HAVE RECOGNIZED BIASES IN our subject access standards—subject headings and classifications—that disadvantage groups of people already disadvantaged in our society through poverty, homelessness, race, ethnicity, disability, age, and other factors.[1] Marielena Fina describes the impact of such bias recalling her 1972 catalog encounter with the Library of Congress subject heading "Libraries and the socially handicapped" while searching for information on Latino library users.[2]

Since then, the institutions governing these standards—the Library of Congress and the Dewey decimal editors and policy committee—have addressed these concerns to varying degrees. In 1986, the Library of Congress changed the aforementioned heading to "Libraries and people with social disabilities" (now seldom used) and added the heading "Hispanic Americans and libraries" along with other specific headings for particular groups. The Dewey decimal classification tries to treat all groups equally (although equal is not always equitable) as shown in efforts to address its Christian bias by moving general works on Christianity out of 201-209 to leave that area free for general religious works. However, other concerns continue; for example, the headings for "Poor" and "Libraries and the poor" would be less dehumanizing if changed to "Poor people" and "Libraries and poor people." Other problems arise from lack of subject headings or classification to express a topic or from faulty application of the standards.

Should individual librarians lobby the Library of Congress and the Dewey establishment to minimize bias? That is certainly one appropriate action. However, it is also appropriate and effective to take some local control. No standard can ever suit every user group in every library. Rural seniors in assisted living facilities may approach topics differently than urban minority college students or new immigrants or social agency workers, but they may all be interested in finding out about renters' rights ("Landlord and tenant"). Those seeking information may not seek assistance from a reference librarian if their search is unsuccessful. The catalog may be their only contact, no matter how approachable librarians are. Therefore, we may need to make additions to records to emphasize local interests and terminology, rather than relying on distant authorities.

Wholesale local revision is not usually economically feasible, but focused adaptation of subject headings for searching and classification for browsing is. It is all about responsibility. We need to hold institutions like Library of Congress and Dewey responsible, but we also need to take responsibility on an everyday, local basis. We have the power in our hands—do we have the will?

NOTES

1. Hope A. Olson and Rose Schlegl, "Standardization, Objectivity, and User Focus: A Meta-Analysis of Subject Access Critiques," *Cataloging & Classification Quarterly* 32, no.2 (2001): 61–80.
2. Marielena Fina, "The Role of Subject Headings in Access to Information: The Experience of One Spanish-Speaking Patron," *Cataloging & Classification Quarterly* 17, no. 1/2 (1993): 267–74.

The Multilingual Materials Acquisition Center

Ingrid Betancourt and Ina Rimpau
Multilingual Materials Acquisition Center
Newark Public Library
Newark, New Jersey

IMMIGRATION IS BRINGING CHANGES TO COM-
munities all over North America, and libraries in previously homogeneous or monolingual communities are striving to meet the needs of these new Americans. The Multilingual Materials Acquisition Center (MultiMAC) at the Newark Public Library in New Jersey is a statewide information clearing-house and resource center for library materials in world languages that help meet these challenges.

MultiMAC's mission is to provide materials, services, and technical assis-tance to libraries serving underserved linguistic groups that represent recent immigration patterns in New Jersey. The center offers services and materials in Arabic, Chinese, Filipino, French, Gujarati, Haitian Creole, Hindi, Korean, Polish, Russian, Spanish, and Vietnamese.

MultiMAC collections include educational, recreational, and informa-tional materials in print, VHS, and audiotape formats. We strive to provide non-English-speaking patrons, young and old alike, with materials that fos-ter their mother cultures, as well as help integrate them into American cul-ture. English as a second language materials, immigration aids, health and parenting information, and current events titles are popular in all languages. Selected lists of titles in all MultiMAC languages can be viewed at www.npl .org/Pages/Multimac/Collections/index.html.

All MultiMAC materials are listed in the Newark Public Library catalog and OCLC's WorldCat, an on-line union catalog. Full cataloging, Romanization of non-Roman scripts, and bilingual subject headings for Spanish are provided. A bilingual librarian does the Spanish cataloging in-house, and we hire freelance catalogers and professional translators as needed. The collections are part of the main library's world languages collection in an easy-to-locate area on the first floor.

Any New Jersey library can request an individual item loan for one month or a bulk loan for three months in increments of 25 up to a total of 100 titles in any one language. This enables libraries to gauge interest in specific languages before committing funds to purchase permanent collections.

Translation services—English into any MultiMAC language, for library services only—are usually requested for library signage, policies, fliers, press releases, and Web pages. The first 500 words of any document are free; subsequent text is charged to the requesting library at commercial rates.

To help library staff meet the challenge of serving diverse linguistic and cultural groups, we offer three staff development workshops: Customer Service in a Multicultural Environment, Developing World Languages Collections, and Marketing the Library in Multicultural Communities. We customize workshops and do on-site consultations as needed.

All of the aforementioned services are free to New Jersey libraries. The center is primarily funded by the federal Library Services and Technology Act grant administered by the New Jersey State Library. The Newark Public Library provides important logistical, supervisory, and financial support.

Uses of Metadata to Expand Access

Jacquie Samples
North Carolina State University
Raleigh, North Carolina

METADATA IS DATA USED TO DESCRIBE AND organize other data in a structured way. It is used to establish database structures, encode content, govern the order of display, and describe the format of data. Metadata also describes how, when, and by whom a particular set of data was collected, brings together preservation and archival data about an object, and allows for the use of such things as thesauri, authority files, subject headings, and locally created subject headings. All of these, in turn, can bring together items in the library catalog, whether they are near each other in library stacks or housed in separate collections. What is most exciting about metadata in the digital age is that it makes information retrieval interactive and flexible.

Metadata is essential for accessing information stored in data warehouses. It facilitates actions upon or about a resource. Libraries worldwide use metadata to enhance their collections in digital and traditional formats by providing access, enhanced information, and unique databases to their users. Many libraries use widely recognized metadata formats such as Dublin Core, MARC21, or EAD to provide these services, while others use homegrown formats.[1]

You use metadata all the time, probably without even knowing it. Any time you limit a search to an author, title, or subject you are taking advantage of the metadata structure and content to access needed materials. Refining a search to get a smaller set of results also relies on the underlying metadata structure. For example, successfully using the "Limit Search" option on on-line database products to find materials published in a specific year requires that the metadata include coding for year of publication. Keyword searching is highly visible to information seekers on the World Wide Web. Web programmers insert keywords, phrases, or even common typographical errors into metadata coding so Internet search engines have a higher probability of listing their sites in a keyword search result.

North Carolina State University Libraries uses metadata to facilitate services to their user communities. Two activities that prominently feature the work of the cataloging department are its participation in NC LIVE and the creation and maintenance of the North Carolina State University Authors Database.

Libraries across North Carolina are attracting more patrons by promoting NC LIVE, which provides free electronic access to full-text articles from over 9,000 newspapers, journals, and magazines; two encyclopedias; and 22,000 electronic books, as well as indexing for 20,000 periodical titles. It can be accessed from an affiliated library or from home.[2] The cataloging department regularly enhances the metadata contained in the university's catalog records for these periodical titles, using locally developed tools to streamline access to NC LIVE resources via the libraries' on-line public access catalog. These tools—the E-Journal Finder and the Database Finder—create indexes of metadata used for e-journals and databases and make them readily available to library users.

The Authors Database offers access to published research being conducted at the university. Database citations represent the published output of faculty, researchers, administrative staff, and students connected with the university since 1997. The cataloging department maintains the database to help collections managers meet faculty and researcher needs. Faculty and departments across campus use the database when writing annual reports and tenure documentation.

Since assuming responsibility for the Authors Database in 1998, the catalog department has been exploring data structures and information delivery models. The database is now accessible through the North Carolina State University catalog. A locally created metadata schema, created with MS

Access software, provides citations of everything written by an author, with links to access points on-line and in the catalog. The metadata schema also streamlines access on the libraries' on-line public access catalog via the Database Finder tool. Most of the items in the Authors Database are held by North Carolina State University Libraries, so the database citations indicate where the items are housed and provide links to electronic versions (when available) via the E-Journal Finder.

The primary role of a library's technical services department can be seen as outreach. As the wardens of the library catalog, both in creation and maintenance, the work of technical services is the foundation of any public service. Public services and technical services should work together to maximize the use and effectiveness of metadata initiatives to address diverse user needs. If public services staff know what patrons are looking for (and how they expect to search for it), technical services staff can determine how to make appropriate resources accessible. Whether they are called upon to modify existing metadata standards or to create a new schema, technical services staff respond to the varied information needs of library users. Together, public and technical services departments can develop tools that ensure equitable access to information for all users, including underrepresented populations such as those who are from culturally diverse backgrounds, speak and read languages other than English, or have limited literacy skills.

NOTES

1. Dublin Core (www.dublincore.org) is the leading international metadata standard for on-line resource discovery. Contributing members seek to develop metadata standards and frameworks that make it easier to find information on the Internet.

    MARC21 (www.loc.gov/marc) stands for the machine-readable cataloging format used to describe resources such as books, journals, and databases. It facilitates cooperative cataloging and data exchange among bibliographic systems. The number 21 designates the most recent version of the standard.

    EAD (www.loc.gov/ead) stands for encoded archival description, a format that archival and cultural heritage institutions use to create digital search aids for their collections.

2. For more information about NC LIVE, visit www.nclive.org/about.phtml.

Planning for System Migration with Input from Staff and Public

Vivian M. Pisano
San Francisco Public Library
San Francisco, California

IN 2000, THE SAN FRANCISCO PUBLIC LIBRARY began preparing to replace its integrated library system. Our patrons needed a system that would serve them better. Our old catalog could not properly display all the diacritical marks and non-Roman characters for materials in languages other than English. Our community is multicultural and multilingual, and we were committed to using an on-line public access catalog (OPAC) that would display non-English language alphabets in truer form. We wanted the Chinese community to view the vernacular scripts that we have provided in our Chinese language bibliographic records, and we wanted to display Roman languages with correct diacritics.

We also wished to expand service to our blind and print-disabled patrons by offering an OPAC for specialized materials. Our old system had a module for circulating these items and for reading selections, but there was no OPAC.

As our first step, we upgraded our infrastructure and equipment. In 2001, we enlisted a library automation consultant and outlined a project timeline, including a detailed schedule of activities. August 2003 was the target date for bringing the system on-line.

A key factor in our two-year venture was staff participation at every step. Staff who work with the public on the desk and in the community could articulate the concerns and needs of their constituents to help us define the ideal system and evaluate the available options. We formed eight committees responsible for identifying functional specifications for the request for proposals (RFP). The committees used a variety of strategies—focus group meetings, interviews, and e-mail solicitations—to get the maximum input from staff members who were not on the committees. The committees posted their work on our staff intranet for review and comment. Some committees invited staff to their meetings to review their reports and to solicit comments and suggestions. We received many useful comments from a wide spectrum of staff.

Summarized documents were converted into an RFP that was issued in January 2002. We received proposals from three vendors and a separate proposal for a stand-alone PC-based blind and print-disabled module. When we evaluated the proposals, we involved library staff at every stage. Vendor demonstrations were presented, with a standard script based on the functional specifications in the RFP. All staff members were invited to attend the demonstrations and to provide feedback. The blind and print-disabled module was demonstrated separately. Another group of staff conducted visits to view the prospective systems on-site in libraries already using the proposed integrated library systems. Questions were posed covering functionality, system performance, dependability, and customer support.

Foremost to the success of the system we would ultimately select would be the public's assessment of the available choices. To solicit public comment, we set up a controlled environment in which we invited the public to review models from the three vendors and to submit written commentary and an overall rating on the functionality of each. These ratings were included in the scores.

Although the process was time-consuming, it was well worth the effort to involve as many people as we did. By helping to define needs and evaluate proposed systems, staff gained an awareness and knowledge of library systems other than the one they had been using for more than 10 years. The comments we received from the formal public commentary session and those we receive on our website have been invaluable in implementing this project. The self-service features and design of the Web OPAC are largely driven by ongoing comments and requests from our users.

BadgerLink: A Statewide License to Learn

Sally Drew
Wisconsin Department of Public
Instruction
Madison, Wisconsin

■ BADGERLINK IS AN OUTREACH INITIATIVE THAT provides access to selected on-line resources for every citizen of Wisconsin. Available to anyone living or working in Wisconsin who has Internet access, BadgerLink offers more than 8,000 magazine, newsletter, newspaper, and reference titles, including the full text of many articles on-line.

BadgerLink is a project of the Division for Libraries, Technology, and Community Learning of the Wisconsin Department of Public Instruction. Its goal is to provide increased access to information resources for Wisconsin residents in cooperation with the state's public, school, academic, and special libraries. The concept of BadgerLink was formulated at the Library Technology Planning Conference in February 1998. Recommendations were put forward to support statewide licensing of on-line databases to promote equal access to information regardless of location. These recommendations formed the core of the goals and objectives of the venture.

BadgerLink services began in July 1998, funded through the Wisconsin Universal Service Fund. The Division for Libraries, Technology, and Community Learning has contracted with two vendors, EBSCO and ProQuest, to provide the resources. The statewide contracts enable Wisconsin residents, libraries, and educational institutions to realize greater cost savings than would be possible through either individual or group contracts. The budget is $1.85 million per year. The BadgerLink site also offers a directory of on-line resources, government sites, and links to WISCAT, the statewide union library catalog for Wisconsin.

To use these resources, you must be a Wisconsin resident or access the materials from a Wisconsin library. User authentication is done by verification of an Internet protocol (IP) address. Wisconsin residents with Internet access can use the magazine and newspaper databases from home if their Internet service provider has registered with the Department of Public Instruction or if their local public library is providing access through a library card or user account. Technical support and training for BadgerLink users is provided by a full-time project coordinator who also maintains a database of IP addresses and works with schools, libraries, and Internet service providers to bring this resource to as many state residents as possible.

BadgerLink provides each citizen with resources for research and doubles as a vital curriculum support for pre-K–12, higher education, and distance education students statewide. Access to these core resources also benefits reference librarians throughout Wisconsin. The commitment to increase equity of access through outreach is a progressive initiative that has served well 24 hours a day for more than five years. BadgerLink is a statewide license to learn.

Creating an Enabling On-line Environment

Axel Schmetzke
University of Wisconsin–Stevens Point

THE MIGRATION OF LIBRARY RESOURCES TO THE on-line environment has created unprecedented opportunities for a highly underserved part of the population: people with print disabilities, who, because of lack of sight, cognitive disabilities (such as dyslexia), or insufficient motor control, cannot independently access printed works. Assistive input and output technology, such as modified computer keyboards and screen readers with speech or Braille output, provides access to electronic text. However, the rapid shift from a text-based to a graphics-based environment threatens to undermine this emerging independence. With pictures, image maps, frames, excessive use of structural markup elements for presentation purposes, and the prominence of distracting glitz, people with print disabilities are at risk of losing their ability to navigate the on-line environment. Even the most advanced assistive devices cannot overcome the barriers associated with inaccessible design.

Librarians seeking to extend services to all potential users need to ensure that on-line resources are accessible. Here are some recommendations:

1. Librarians must educate themselves about on-line accessibility issues.

My own Accessible Web Design Resources page (http://library.uwsp.edu/ aschmetz/Accessible/pub_resources.htm) is one of several links to information for both beginning and advanced learners. Those preferring a more structured setting can choose from a variety of on-line courses, such as those offered by EASI (http://easi.cc/workshop.htm). Axslib (www.rit.edu/~easi/ lists.htm), an on-line discussion forum on accessibility-related library issues, provides up-to-date information as well as ad hoc advice.

2. Librarians have to ensure that their own institutional Web pages are accessible. This includes designing new pages in compliance with the Web Content Accessibility Guidelines (WCAG)[1] or the Access Board standards issued under section 508 of the Rehabilitation Act of 1973,[2] checking existing pages for accessibility, and making corrections when necessary. Bobby and Lynx Viewer, while not perfect, are valuable checking tools.[3] The Web Accessibility Initiative's Quick Tips Reference Card (www.w3.org/WAI/ References/QuickTips/) is particularly useful for Web design novices.[4]

3. Librarians need to incorporate accessibility clauses into all policies that involve on-line resources and services. For example, collection development policies should specifically include accessibility as one of the criteria to be considered when selecting vendor-provided resources.

4. Librarians should also urge vendors to make accessible products. "ADA-compliant" is far too vague. Compliance with the Web Content Accessibility Guidelines or section 508 is good. Demonstrated product usability by people with disabilities (such as screen reader users) is even better. Requesting the company's published accessibility policy accentuates the importance of the issue.

5. Finally, librarians can ensure that the policies issued by their professional organizations promote Web accessibility. For example, the latest edition of the Association of College & Research Libraries' Guidelines for Distance Learning Library Services needs revision. Nowhere does it address accessibility for students with disabilities.[5]

To a large extent, disability is socially constructed. By this I mean that whether individuals with disabilities can pursue independent and fulfilling lives is not merely a matter of their particular internal conditions, but is also a question of enabling or disabling external factors put in place by society and its institutions. By removing barriers from their Web pages, by considering accessibility when selecting electronic resources, by challenging vendors to make more accessible products, and by adopting policies that seek to realize the opportunities new information technology provides, libraries can create the conditions that would enable all people, including those with "disabilities," to participate fully in the evolving information society.

NOTES

1. The Web Content Accessibility Guidelines (WCAG) explain how to design Web pages so that their content is accessible to people with disabilities. The guidelines were developed in 1999 by the Web Accessibility Initiative, which was sponsored by the World Wide Web Consortium, an international standard-setting body. The guidelines and a companion Checklist of Checkpoints are located at www.w3.org/TR/WCAG10 and at www.w3.org/TR/WCAG10/full-checklist.html, respectively. A revised set of guidelines, WCAG 2.0, is under review.
2. Section 508 is a provision within the Rehabilitation Act of 1973, as amended by Congress in 1998, that mandates that electronic and information technology developed, maintained, procured, or used by the U.S. government must be accessible to people with disabilities. To make section 508 enforceable, the Architectural and Transformation Barriers Compliance Board ("Access Board") published detailed accessibility standards for such products (www.access-board.gov/sec508/508standards.htm).
3. Bobby is a program that helps designers check if their Web pages are in conformance with either the Web Content Accessibility Guidelines or the access standards issued under section 508. A simple online Bobby version is available for free at http://bobby.watchfire.com/bobby/html/en/index.jsp. Lynx Viewer (www.delorie.com/web/lynxview.html) allows Web authors to see what their pages look like when viewed with Lynx, a text-only browser.
4. For further accessible Web design tips and other related resources, visit the author's Accessible Webpage Design Resources page at http://library.uwsp.edu/aschmetz/Accessible/pub_resources.htm.
5. www.ala.org/Content/NavigationMenu/ACRL/Standards_and_Guidelines/Guidelines_for_Distance_Learning_Library_Services.htm.

Expanding Access to Collections through Digitization

Ewa Barczyk and Krystyna Matusiak
University of Wisconsin–Milwaukee
Libraries

THE UNIVERSITY OF WISCONSIN-MILWAUKEE (UWM) has a unique mission called the Milwaukee Idea that commits the university to engage with the community in partnerships that "enhance the quality of life for all." The UWM Libraries support this mission by sharing our resources with the community. In fall of 2001 the libraries created an on-line library of digital collections that was conceived in partnerships with community agencies and faculty members.

The goal of the program is to share the libraries' unique and valuable collections with a wider audience who may not otherwise have access to the original collections. UWM Libraries staff assessed proposals for this project, posing the following questions:

Which of our resources are unique and difficult to access?

Which resources have preservation needs?

Which of these collections have faculty used in their curricula?

Do we have intellectual property rights for those items?

Who are potential partners in the community and on campus?

Since the inception of the program four distinct digital collections have been created that provide remote access to visual resources on global issues as well as treasures of local cultural heritage.

First, in response to the tragic events of September 11 and the ongoing war in Afghanistan, the libraries created an on-line photo exhibition called "Afghanistan: Images from the Harrison Forman Collection." The collection consists of 186 images selected from more than 80,000 slides at the Harrison Forman Photographic Collection housed at the American Geographical Society Library at UWM. The photographs, taken in 1969, show Afghanistan as a stable, thriving country. Some of the more striking images include those of Afghan families and children, women dressed in traditional clothing, workers engaged in local trades, and two 1,500-year-old Buddha statues later destroyed by the Taliban. The collection received national attention and was selected as Yahoo! Editors' Choice in April 2002. The collection also received an award from Education World, a website for educators.

The second project, "Milwaukee Repertory Theater Photographic History," is a collaboration between the Milwaukee community and the libraries. The on-line collection provides a visual chronicle of the 195 productions of the Milwaukee Repertory Theater from 1977 to 1994. More than 1,800 images were selected from the Mark Avery Collection housed in the UWM Libraries' archives, providing the only means of access to this rich cultural resource. The images are indexed extensively by play title, author name, season, actors' names, and names of additional contributing artists in order to provide additional points of access in the searchable collection. Staff from the theater assisted in the metadata creation by identifying unnamed actors in the slides.

"Transportation around the World: 1911–1993" undertakes a global theme and shares 650 unique images from the photographic collections of the American Geographical Society Library. The photographs present various modes of transportation used in 79 countries. They are indexed by transportation type, mode, facility, and geographic location. The topic for this project was suggested by faculty in the School of Architecture for use with college and K–12 students.

The most recent digital project, "Milwaukee Neighborhoods," shows the development of city neighborhoods in the twentieth century. Many images are from the Roman Kwasniewski Photographic Collection that documents lives of Polish immigrants on Milwaukee's South Side. Other images come from the Harold Mayer Collection and from nineteenth century monographs about Milwaukee that include German immigrant contributions. The images are accompanied by maps showing the changes in neighborhoods through-out the city.

UWM Libraries' digital collections can be accessed at www.uwm.edu/Library/digilab. The website also includes links to digital collections created in collaboration with other University of Wisconsin libraries. These links provide access to unique resources that are otherwise hidden from most users.

PART 5

Advocacy and Outreach: A Natural Connection

Maureen O'Connor
Queens Borough Public Library
Jamaica, New York

■ ADVOCACY IS A BUZZWORD IN THE LIBRARY world today. You can see this when you review library literature, look at websites of professional organizations, or glance at staff development calendars and conference programs. We must advocate for support of library services, and we need to draw that support from the public, press, government, and funding sources. Outreach librarians are uniquely positioned to do so. As a matter of course, we meet with the public, community groups, and government officials in order to develop programs and services for target populations. These opportunities for networking and visibility should enable us to represent libraries to different audiences in new ways and to advocate for equitable service for all library users.

However, outreach librarians often have to work hard internally to convince colleagues, administrators, and trustees of the value of providing library services to special populations. This is especially true when funding is tight and outreach falls outside "core services." But the same director who views outreach as an add-on that falls outside traditional library services knows who to call when a local newspaper or legislator needs a human interest story to demonstrate how the library impacts the community.

Our challenge is complex. How can we, as outreach advocates, tell and sell the value of our services to our profession, to the public, to the target groups we serve, and to policy makers? This multifaceted approach is necessary if we intend to improve the quality of library service for all. To be successful, outreach services need to be systematized and incorporated into a library's service plan. All people deserve quality library services, and these services can't rely upon the zeal of one librarian or on short-lived grant funds. Outreach staff need career ladders. Services must be supported with realistic funding. An overriding question is how do we attain this goal of incorporation?

ATTEND MEETINGS

The first step is to get out the door, to meet with local organizations that share a service mission and customer base. We need to be at the table when services for a particular population in our community are discussed. We need to be there to determine the library's role in meeting community needs, not have it defined without us or, even worse, never considered. My advice is to make the first move—don't wait for an invitation.

Librarians are trained to find information, and we must use those skills to identify key contacts in our community. Make cold calls to set up meetings with key individuals or organizations. Get schedules for meetings of groups you'd like to work with and ask if you can attend. Remember, if no one from the library is at the table, policy makers may not think about library service. If you are there you'll often be included. It may not happen the first time, but it will happen if you persevere.

Admittedly, this can be difficult. Allocating human resources to strengthen our presence at community meetings runs counter to the current trend toward expanding websites and on-line resources for people to access library services from home.

LISTEN AND LEARN

Some meetings are better than others. You may find the wrong group but meet one person who made your time worthwhile. Or you may find the right group but the wrong agenda. Movers and shakers are in the room, but today's topic is irrelevant to you. Stay with it—you'll learn something. If the group consists of representatives from agencies that serve the population you're interested in reaching, you'll eventually connect. Librarians often lament that other professions know little about libraries. That may be true, but it goes both ways. I can't decipher mental health acronyms and am lost in the intricacies of welfare reform. But that's all right. You can ask questions, listen, and learn. You don't need all the details, but you do need a grasp of the issues and policies involved. What is important is that you know your library services and consider how they can address the issue being discussed.

Another issue is individual comfort level. It's easier to walk into a meeting filled with other librarians or people you're already affiliated with, those who share your experience and point of view, than a roomful of strangers. But those strangers may be people you need to know. They might be able to assist with funding, recruitment, and promotion of library service to your target population.

THINK ABOUT LIBRARY CONNECTIONS

Meeting with strangers is a lot like public speaking. The more you do it, the better you'll get. Advocates are noted for being good speakers. More important, they're good listeners. When you're meeting with a group for the first time, are you asked to be on the agenda and to give a brief talk about the library? Do your best to avoid this. Stall. Libraries provide a tremendous array of services. You need to get familiar enough with the group and its issues to tailor your talk to your audience. For example, a few years ago I attended a statewide conference of outreach coordinators, agencies, and advocates for the aging. Librarians came prepared to talk about services to the homebound, but senior services personnel were interested in Internet training for their clients and programs held at libraries because they provided van service. Libraries were well able to provide the services requested, but the services requested weren't what the librarians in attendance expected.

Listening to other attendees gives you clues to what's important to the audience. Often what's important to them may not be what the library considers its outstanding attribute. Seek a balance between taking nothing for granted and burying people in paper and statistics. Most people know something about libraries, but their knowledge may be from years ago or from their personal use of one library. They may have no idea of the multitude of services beyond checking out bestsellers.

THINK ABOUT COLLABORATIONS

Not much is free today, and that's a big selling point for libraries, but how many of us state that up front? Librarians are information specialists, so we read more than most people. Librarians expect handouts, but many other groups don't. I suggest that you spend more time attending meetings and preparing remarks than producing another piece of paper.

Meeting the key players in your community can lead to exciting partnerships that benefit the library and the public. Partnerships are developed when groups identify mutual interests and a common mission, and realize how their services can be complementary. Grants offer excellent opportunities to forge partnerships because they are often part of a grant's requirements. Collaboration is a cost-effective, broad-based way to deliver services and can bring in money for library services. The goal is to be at the table when preliminary discussions about grant proposals take place, not to be asked for a letter of support as an afterthought.

In Queens, the administrators of the public hospitals and the Queens Borough Public Library realized they served the same people and faced similar problems serving a diverse multilingual population. Both have learned and benefited from their partnership.

We need to go beyond advocacy to become players in our communities. I was at a meeting recently where Joey Rodger, executive director of the Urban Libraries Council, made a distinction between community advocates and players. Advocates, she said, often have but one message: "library, library, library." Players, on the other hand, show up and talk about children, jobs, community safety, health, or whatever issues the gathering is addressing. That really sums it up. If we become players in our communities, we can learn how the library is relevant to pressing issues. Outreach librarians operate in the broader context of society and public policy. We need to optimize our knowledge of that context.

My New Year's resolution for 2004 was to be more selective about which meetings I attend. I want to change the ratio of internal library meetings versus community meetings at which I am an outsider but could be a player.

There are many well-established networks serving and advocating for people we also want to serve, often identified as special populations: inmates, low-literate residents, immigrants, and the unemployed. Let's take advantage of these networks, of their visibility and clout, and find out how libraries can support their initiatives. There is strength in numbers. The following articles describe how libraries have successfully used advocacy through partnerships, demographics, the media, and local government to build support for their libraries and to better serve targeted populations. Together we can meet a common goal of providing equitable library services for all.

Sisterfriends@Your Library: Marketing and Building Support for Programs

LaToya McLean
Public Library of Charlotte and
Mecklenburg County
Charlotte, North Carolina

IN 2001, THE PUBLIC LIBRARY OF CHARLOTTE and Mecklenburg County launched a program for women that is a book club, empowerment group, and source of information all rolled into one. Sisterfriends@Your Library was created in direct response to patrons asking for more programs geared to women's issues. Sisterfriends uses literature to give women a forum for sharing their experiences and discussing issues that are important to them. The program carves out a time for them to take care of their body and soul so that they, in turn, can take care of their families, careers, and daily responsibilities. With support of good promotion and marketing, Sisterfriends has been very well received. In fact, it was so popular that the library expanded the program to women in the local jail.

At the library, Sisterfriends meetings include aromatherapy candles and tranquility fountains to encourage relaxation and a retreat from the pressures of day-to-day life. At the jail, where such accessories are not allowed, a sound spa duplicates the sounds of nature and fragrant sachets create a soothing atmosphere similar to that of the meetings held at the library.

In the book discussion component, women who participate at the jail read the same books as the Sisterfriends group at the library. They also write book reviews for our Sisterfriends and Readers' Club websites. In 2003, several inmates had their work published in *Hungry for Home,* a book of regional recipes and stories published by Novello Festival Press, an imprint of the Public Library of Charlotte and Mecklenburg County.

A strategic media and marketing campaign has been indispensable to the program's success with the general public and jail inmates. Marketing includes radio spots, direct mailings, conferences, word-of-mouth communication, fliers, brochures, articles in *Check It Out,* the library's monthly newsletter, cross-promotion with similar library programs, and reminder e-mails to participants one week before each program. These efforts have heightened awareness of Sisterfriends and boosted attendance at individual programs.

Here are a few additional promotional tips that have helped Sisterfriends build its audience.

> Court the media. Send a short press release or a special invitation to your event, and follow up with a phone call. Inviting members of the media to emcee programs has boosted Sisterfriends' attendance and may work for your programs as well.

> Mine your data. Have everyone sign in. Get names, addresses, phone numbers, and e-mail addresses so you can send out information about future events. You might also want to include space for ideas for future discussions. Have plenty of literature about upcoming events on hand.

> Partner with businesses. One Sisterfriends bookstore partner provides free books for the program at the jail. The bookstore is also an excellent outlet for program brochures, signs, and other promotional material.

> Contact publishers. By working with publishers, Sisterfriends organizers were able to arrange groundbreaking author visits to the jail program. Writers signed books, mingled with the inmates, and conducted writing workshops.

Marketing and promotion helped to develop and expand the targeted audience for Sisterfriends@Your Library. With some planning and legwork—and little or no money—librarians around the country can achieve similar success for their programs.

Outreach Starts at the Top: Advice from a Library Director

Dinah Smith O'Brien
Plymouth Public Library
Plymouth, Massachusetts

IF IT WALKS LIKE A DUCK AND QUACKS LIKE A duck, it must be a duck, right? Simple logic, but too limited in the world of library directors. Libraries are living, breathing organisms, and any library service is an outreach service. Walls have come down, virtual catalogs abound, and definitions have changed. The traditional approaches to outreach—bookmobiles, senior housing collections, and serving the needs of the underserved—are no longer applicable. They are not even the beginning!

In my role as library director, I like to think of outreach in a new light. Webster defines outreach as "to surpass in reach; to go too far; to exceed traditional limits." This is why I wanted to be at the top—to demonstrate the vision and the leadership to go that extra mile, to think outside the box.

We all have our own beliefs, but I would wager that upon entering library school each of us had a deep-seated desire to connect people with information. If you went into library administration, as I did, you probably also believed that you had the ability to lead, persuade, mentor, and coach. Combine this ability with a true dedication to public service and you have a solid foundation "to exceed traditional limits." As a director, you must have the ability to effect change, to work with a board to establish policy, and to connect with your staff. You should also have a pretty good idea about what drives the community you serve and how the community views your institution.

Remember that the patrons we serve identify the entire staff with the library. This is apparent when a staff member goes to the local supermarket and folks start asking him or her library questions. Our customers identify all of us as librarians, MLS or not. And this public perception must be acknowledged, for it is what defines our libraries. Every staff member must be trained for outreach. Professional staff may want to go into specialty areas such as reader's advisory or services to seniors, children, or adults, but nine out of ten times it is the frontline paraprofessional staff who represent your institution. Patrons in the stacks ask pages who are shelving to help them find books. Circulation technicians see 99 percent of all people who cross the threshold. Custodians often know where more things are in your building than you do! All staff members are dong outreach, so make sure they understand why and how. Train them.

Frontline staff and, okay, even catalogers: you need to remember the "Library Blue Rule" in the gospel according to Dinah. Just because your director may not have identified all services in your library as outreach does not mean they aren't outreach services. Remember that in the gilded book on care and feeding of your library director, the main thing is to make the director look good! This is accomplished by providing outreach in every way you can. In most medium-sized and larger libraries patrons are more familiar with you than they are with the director. You represent the library, at all times! Find out how you can improve customer service, go that extra mile, and listen, listen, listen. And on the flip side, ask, ask, *ask* for support you need to do what you love to do.

Don't lose sight of why you work for the library, whether as frontline staff, librarian, or director: to ensure that the customer is served and served well. Money, training, time, and resources are essential to support outreach. Don't be afraid to reach too far to meet your customers' needs.

A special note to directors: lead by example. Reach out to your staff with the training they need to do good community outreach, and reach out to your community with good library services. Believe me, they will reach back to you. If you talk the talk of a library leader, you must also walk the walk. Outreach begins at the top. Outreach begins with you.

Advocating for Library Services in County Facilities

Sharon Holley
Buffalo and Erie County Public Library
Buffalo, New York

THE PROVISION OF LIBRARY SERVICES TO county facilities demonstrates how libraries can advocate for diverse residents in cooperation with other county-funded agencies. Providing these services also benefits library advocacy efforts within Erie County, New York.

Buffalo and Erie County Public Library is a county-based library system with a commitment to serving all of its residents, including those who are institutionalized. Through its outreach efforts, the library system has developed a role in the arenas of criminal justice and senior services, and these efforts go a long way toward confirming the value of the library to the community. County legislators who determine library funding hear about its services from a variety of voices beyond traditional public library advocates.

The Buffalo and Erie County Public Library has a long history of serving residents of Erie County's nursing home, jail, and holding center. It works to ensure that services to those facilities replicate those available in neighborhood branch libraries as much as possible. The institutional services are sustained through the library's ongoing funding of paid staff positions. Librarians and clerical staff at the facilities are employees of the Buffalo and Erie County Public Library who work in its institutions division, a unit within the

Department of Extension Services. In order to maintain coverage and continuity during vacations or sick leave, extension services staff are trained to work at each facility—so that service is never interrupted by vacation, sick leave, etc. Materials budgets for each of these institutions are monitored by library staff, who also process orders.

The branch library at the county nursing home in Alden opened in 1956 with only a few books, but it has evolved dramatically. Its users—seniors and people with disabilities—enjoy typical branch services as well as coffee hour, read-aloud programs, and travel clubs. Four computers are on hand for residents to use, and residents meet weekly with a volunteer facilitator to discuss current events. Magnifying bars, book supports, tape players, slides, slide viewers, and electronic magnifiers are available. Collections of large-print books, videotapes, and spoken word books create a warm place to find information or just sit and talk to a friend. Room-to-room cart service is provided to those who cannot come to the library. The branch is currently staffed by a senior library clerk, a page, and an army of loyal volunteers.

The library within the Erie County Correctional Facility in Alden, also started in 1956, has developed into a self-contained entity. Through scheduled visits, inmates are provided access to books, serials, typewriters, tape players, and computers. Special collections include African American history, adventure, and street fiction. A law library occupying nearly one-third of the library is available for legal research. Inmates are able to request materials that are available in the library system but not housed at the branch. A full-time librarian II and six inmate workers currently staff the branch.

The holding center library began in 1969 as cart service to cells. It has grown to encompass a new facility with both a legal collection and a general library. Residents can borrow all types of materials, from adventure fiction to religious nonfiction, and can use a large legal collection while awaiting trial. This branch is currently staffed by a senior library clerk and four residents.

The Department of Extension Services also provides a youth book collection at the new Youth Detention Center. Library staff coordinate with teaching staff to provide recreational and academic materials. A satellite collection of popular paperbacks has also been placed in the jury room of the Erie County courthouse.

These programs of the Department of Extension Services affirm the Buffalo and Erie County Public Library's commitment to providing quality library services to diverse members of our communities. They also demonstrate the value of these services to our trustees and county officials. We are walking and talking advocates for equity of access.

Cultural Ambassadors Program: Putting the World within Reach

Susan McCarthy
Arlington County Public Library
Arlington, Virginia

ARLINGTON COUNTY PUBLIC LIBRARY CREATED three goals to market library collections, services, and programs to its community:

1. to proactively promote our range of library services and resources rather than wait for customers to come to us
2. to know more about the community we serve and which of our library services could be beneficial to our patrons
3. to build a solid base of constituent services (i.e., to be at the table or to be in the minds of community partners when decisions are made)

The phrase we use to promote this concept is "putting the world within reach." The library established two programs to achieve our goals: the Cultural Ambassadors Program, which establishes staff liaisons with new immigrant populations, and the Partnerships Program, which engages professional staff with a variety of community organizations.

The Cultural Ambassadors Program was created to establish connections with new Latino and Ethiopian immigrants living in Arlington. According to Census 2000, about 28 percent of Arlington County residents are foreign-born. Salvadorans and other Latin American immigrants form the largest group, followed by North Africans from Ethiopia and Somalia. Library staff who are members of these communities and who are fluent in appropriate languages volunteered to be the liaisons. Two Spanish-speaking staff and one Ethiopian staff member, speaking Amharic, are the primary contacts for reaching out to these language communities.

Ambassadors meet regularly with a wide range of community agencies, from Hispanics Against Child Abuse and Neglect to the Ethiopian Community Development Center. They inform their respective communities about relevant library programs and services. The ambassadors help plan for celebratory events at the library, attend cultural events in the community, and conduct Spanish language book discussion groups. Their names and phone numbers appear on all publicity materials for special events in the target communities. The ambassador puts a name and face on library service, a personal contact for members of these cultural groups.

Ambassadors reach people in the community by many methods. They developed a Spanish language media contact list, ran ads in the Ethiopian yellow pages, and placed articles in Ethiopian ethnic newspapers to promote awareness of the library.

The Partnership Program focused on getting staff out of the library and establishing partnerships with community agencies. In 2003, all professional staff were required to collaborate with a civic, school, professional community, faith-based, or social service organization. They were required to dedicate a minimum of 16 hours over the year. The direct contact enabled staff to learn about community resources and to share information about library resources. Some partnerships grew into successful collaborations and established ongoing relationships for mutual benefit in our community.

A partnership handbook, now converted to Web pages on the library's intranet, provides the foundation for ongoing staff partnerships and ambassadorships. A welcome folder and a family of library publications allow staff to tailor packets to individual organizations. Staff members report their contacts to a database so that measures can be captured. Last year, 40 participating library staff made 199 separate contacts to 95 organizations. As a result of these programs, the library is more active in local community activities, more aware of community issues, and better able to focus its collections and services. Our customer base continues to grow as people become aware of library resources. We have seen a 5 percent increase in annual circulation and a 6 percent increase in program attendance.

Libraries and Literacy: Making New Connections

Roberta Reiss
Collier County Public Library
Naples, Florida

SOME LIBRARY OUTREACH SPECIALISTS DESIGN their programs based on the philosophy "build it and they will come." In today's environment of limited resources, minimal staffing, and growing underserved populations, I prefer deep and far-reaching conversations with potential partners and targeted patrons. Programs designed in the relative quiet of my office can look good on paper, incorporating all the elements of successful outreach. But a reality check that involves field research, discussion, and collaboration with partners increases my chances of creating a successful program with measurable outcomes.

I manage a volunteer tutoring program for Collier County Public Library in Naples, Florida. The program offers one-on-one and small-group instruction to adults who want to improve their reading and English language skills. We train our own tutors as well as those who volunteer at the many literacy organizations throughout Collier and Lee counties. We also maintain an adult literacy lending collection for tutors, adult learners, and new readers. With grant funding, we recently began offering English language instruction in dedicated computer labs at several branch locations.

Collier is a large, diverse county that includes resorts, retirement and golf course communities, low-income housing, and agricultural areas. Service industries comprise a large percentage of our economic base. Many service industry employees have long commutes, often sharing rides or using employer-provided transportation. Most of our tutors and learners meet at library branches for their lessons. After several years of operation, we realized that many of our learners faced several obstacles making participation in our program difficult, if not impossible. Their biggest hurdle turned out to be transportation. Missing your ride home to have an English or reading lesson makes it hard to commit to a course of study!

To address these barriers we initiated an outreach program that offers workplace literacy training in partnership with local hotels, hospitals, continuing care facilities, and gated communities. We approached local employers with a proposal to include literacy lessons in employee training. Our pitch focused on the bottom-line benefits to the employer: improved customer service, better supervisor-employee communication, safety, and, last but not least, media attention and positive community relations. The basic contract with employers was that we provide or train tutors and employers provide meeting space, materials, and employee incentives.

Meetings with human resource managers, activities directors, club board members, and mid-level supervisors were critical for planning logistics and identifying potential participants. Creating lesson plans relevant to the workplace involved design meetings with training managers and informal surveys asking employees the question, What would you like to learn to make you more confident on the job? In situations where employees volunteered to tutor other employees, or residents volunteered to tutor caregivers and lawn maintenance personnel, we scheduled on-site tutor training and ordered materials.

The result? Well-attended classes, happy supervisors, satisfied customers, fulfilled tutors, and confident employees. Success stories abound, especially in our partnerships with continuing care facilities. Employees gain the skills to move from housekeeping to dining room to certified nursing assistant positions. As for me, I have the satisfaction of identifying a need, empowering the participants, and serving the underserved.

New Americans Program: Outreach through Partnerships

Adriana Acauan Tandler
Queens Borough Public Library
Jamaica, New York

RECENTLY, THE QUEENS BOROUGH PUBLIC Library held a program on diabetes in one of our branches. It was part of our collaboration with the Queens Health Network, which consists of two public hospitals and satellite clinics in Queens to provide health information to the community. To reach our target population, the entire program was conducted in Spanish. The doctor spoke in Spanish about diabetes, and handouts and book displays were in Spanish. Hospital staff then screened the twenty-five attendees and found two in need of immediate medical attention. The doctor spoke with both privately and they agreed to be at the clinic the following Monday.

This example illustrates the benefits of partnerships, especially in places like Queens, one of five counties in New York City and the most ethnically diverse county in the United States.[1] To meet the challenge of serving immigrants, the Queens Borough Public Library used grant funds to initiate the New Americans Project in 1977. The project has been integrated into the library's services since 1982 and is now known as the New Americans Program. The library's collaboration with the Queens Health Network is just one example of how the program has made a positive difference in the community.

When planning programs and collections for immigrant groups in Queens, we keep two facts in mind. First, most immigrants are not accustomed to using the library for information critical to their lives. In order to be effective in attracting immigrants, the library must seek assistance. Partnering with other agencies has been pivotal to the success of the New Americans Program in reaching and serving immigrants.

The first step in reaching immigrants is to find out where they come from, what languages they speak, and where they live. Census data and information from city planning and health departments have helped us identify nationalities and languages by service areas. The next step is to align ourselves and establish partnerships with agencies that serve the groups we have identified. These partnerships range from formal contracts to informal agreements. Potential partners are unlimited as long as there is a commonality of mission, goals, and philosophy in serving immigrants. Partners are great sources of performers and speakers, of help in promoting programs, and very importantly, of input on cultural differences and which issues are a priority for their constituents.

For example, to reach the Korean community, we organized a meeting of Korean social workers. They recommended that we conduct a program on child abuse prevention but in order to establish an acceptable level of comfort they advised us not to mention child abuse on the promotional flyer. This was valuable input. Not only did the group provide us with a Korean speaker to lead the program "Overcoming Our Worries about Our Children," they identified a priority issue and advised how to frame it so as not offend the group we wanted to attract.

The New Americans Program has partnered with hundreds of organizations over the years. Initially, library staff did all the outreach, but now we are the ones being approached. These partnerships have enabled the library to increase the number and kinds of services we provide, and we, in turn, have been able to help agencies reach some immigrants who may not be aware of their services.

To potential partners we stress that libraries are dynamic community and learning centers that can provide resources for lifelong learning. Through partnerships we can be more effective. For both library and partner, the benefit is an increase in the number of people served with the cost efficiency of shared resources. In this equation there are only winners, and the biggest winner of all is the customer.

NOTE

1. Suketu Mehta, "The Meltingest Pot," *New York Times Magazine*, October 5, 2003, 88.

World Language Collections: Mining Demographic Data

A. Issac Pulver
Shaker Heights Public Library
Shaker Heights, Ohio

Joan Clark
Cleveland Public Library
Cleveland, Ohio

THE CLEVELAND PUBLIC LIBRARY HAS A DIStinguished history of reaching out to new groups arriving in the city. The Main Library's foreign literature department consists of about 250,000 volumes in 45 languages and circulates more books than any other department. The department's relationship with agencies that serve immigrants, particularly the International Services Center, accounts for much of its success.

In 2000, the foreign literature department began to examine its circulation figures in relationship to the census and to other statistical information in order to determine where extra outreach and programming efforts were needed. Some data indicated changes were necessary to ensure that all of the city's citizens were served.

The overwhelming circulation leaders in the department's non-English language materials are those in Russian (50 percent) and Chinese (25 percent), with Spanish language materials a distant third (5 percent). In the census, however, 0.5 percent of respondents identified themselves as being of Russian ancestry; another 0.4 percent self-identified as Chinese, and a comparatively overwhelming 7.3 percent self-identified as Hispanic or Latino.

The raw numbers suggested that circulation of Spanish materials should be much higher.

The department was determined to develop strategies to reach out to this underserved group. Using demographics as a starting point, the department put forth the following hypotheses about library use among Cleveland's Spanish speakers.

- Cleveland's Spanish speakers are bilingual, so they are not dependent on the Spanish language collection.

- Spanish-speaking newcomers may be arriving from countries with low literacy rates.

- Cleveland's Spanish speakers get their information and entertainment from other media.

- The foreign literature department does not collect the kinds of materials Spanish readers want.

- The department's outreach methods overlook Spanish-speaking newcomers.

- The Spanish-speaking community had arrived too recently to have an impact on library circulation.

- Spanish-speaking newcomers are arriving from countries that do not have a well-developed culture of library use.

Several of the hypotheses proved true, but others did not.

- According to the census, nearly 60 percent of Cleveland's Spanish speakers also speak English; the same is true of those who speak other Indo-European languages.

- Seventy-five percent of Cleveland's Hispanic residents are from Puerto Rico, which has an illiteracy rate of 2 percent, twice the U.S. average but similar to China's 2.3 percent.

- Cleveland has several Spanish-language radio and television stations and newspapers.

- The foreign literature department's collection development practices always emphasized quality over popularity and literature over nonfiction.

- By depending upon its relationship with the International Services Center, which serves immigrants and refugees, the department was missing the overwhelming number of recently arrived Hispanics from Puerto Rico.

- The Hispanic community in Cuyahoga County grew by 50 percent between 1990 and 2000.
- A 1994 study by the International Federation of Library Associations and Institutions found that, with few exceptions, very little data about library use is gathered in Latin America.

The foreign literature department drew upon these findings to develop two strategies for meeting the needs of the region's rapidly growing Hispanic population. One is to broaden collection development practices to include more popular materials, including translations of fiction into Spanish and a variety of life skills materials. The second strategy entails partnering with community agencies that are not traditionally associated with immigrants or refugees but that serve, or wish to serve, the Hispanic community.

Most importantly, instigated by the foreign literature department's efforts, the library's administration recognized the importance of Cleveland's growing Hispanic community. Improving services to this segment of our population is identified as a priority in its current strategic plan.

PART 6

Staff Development: Assessing Our Own Behaviors

Sandra Ríos Balderrama
RíosBalderrama Consulting
Scottsdale, Arizona

ON THE FIRST DAY OF MY FIRST JOB OUT OF library school—as a children's librarian—I was welcomed by branch manager Cecellia Shearron-Hawkins. With the sunlight streaming in through the windows of the closed branch she sat across from me, one-on-one, at a table on the public floor. Her first words expressed the great respect she had for the skills, education, expertise, and training of children's librarians. She told me that she looked forward to working together for and with the multicultural community of south Berkeley (Calif.). This vivid memory of that day in 1986 set the tone for my own choices and decisions as to how I would approach my future work as a public service librarian, branch manager, district supervisor, recruiter, trainer, learner, consultant, mentor, and mentee.

Through Cecellia's modeling I learned what mutual respect and reciprocation looked like between colleagues with different skills, different scopes of responsibility, different designations of authority, different perspectives, different approaches to work, and even different cultural experiences and reference points. Her communication skills were open, consistent, and constructive. She was an intent listener and learner. Although I deferred to her authority at the branch with respect, I felt respected as a staff member with experience and potential. To her I was a welcome arrival with a life full of experience and potential. I was not a blank slate. I was immediately considered part of the team with my distinctive skills that—with the community—would design and implement the shared vision of library service. I worked with Cecellia for three years. This essay is dedicated to her.

In my subsequent years and journeys as a librarian and as a consultant, I realize that my early crossroad with Cecellia may have been atypical. I have borne sacred witness to people's stories of frustration, disrespect, lack of recognition, lack of opportunity for development or advancement, lack of accessibility to management, and lack of a simple "hello" by coworkers in the morning. Libraries were experienced as organizations of distrust, elitism, hierarchy, racism, sexism, homophobia, ageism, divisions between departments and job classifications, "stuffiness," and low morale.

I learned that it was the service to the public that kept library workers going. It was the beloved community with which library workers developed mutual rapport, respect, and reciprocation that gave reward. It was the collections that library workers selected, developed, and cataloged based on patron needs and interests that gave satisfaction. If one could not contribute to the development of themselves, their colleagues, or their organizational culture, then it felt easier to "silo" yourself and keep focused on service outside. After all, service is what library patrons depend on. Some administrators and staff disagreed with the criticisms of our internal workplaces. These administrators and staff believed that through our work—from collection development to multicultural programming, to outreach services, to increasing access via automation and technical services—libraries are fair, balanced, and accessible to all, even employees.

In my most recent career as a recruiter I have found that job seekers are interested in opportunities to learn, to advance, and to contribute. Staff development and staff recognition programs are considered priorities as they look for work. The organizational culture of the library is considered. Potential applicants ask:

> What is the management style of library managers?
>
> What is the library's record on diversity—internally and externally?

Can a person move up or at least laterally—in order to experience new patrons and learn new skills?

What are the training and staff development opportunities?

As an employer it is tempting to answer these questions quickly in the affirmative. However, if any of us paused and reflected on the current status of our library, the answers might very well begin with: "Well . . . sometimes" or "It depends on who you work for" or "That's fine as long as you keep it low profile" or "We tried that already." The most valuable response any employer can give is an honest one. Any job seeker knows that there is no perfect library, but if the library has a track record of working toward specific goals of employee satisfaction in the workplace and employee development then it has a better chance at successful recruitment.

In this chapter you will find a diversity of library advocates—some of them working in libraries and some of them working with libraries—who write about applying outreach skills inward. They suggest—as do I—that we need to look in a mirror to assess our own behaviors and commitments. As we outreach to the community, let us in-reach to ourselves. Outreach skills are based on how to relate to other people beyond our own familiarity and comfort zone. They involve diversifying strategies to make that connection with other people on behalf of a larger goal or vision. That goal might be enlightening one's self as opposed to someone else. It might be increasing access to resources and opportunities. It might be sharing the responsibility for learning how to communicate with one another in an age of diversity where there is no longer a mainstream.

Outreach skills are indispensable when it comes to training each other, learning from each other, measuring the effectiveness of our services, recruiting and hiring, and creating integral staff development plans. We must use outreach skills to support outreach services as well as strengthen the internal health of our libraries as workplaces and learning organizations.

Developing Outreach Skills in Library Staff

Yolanda J. Cuesta
Cuesta Multicultural Consulting
Sacramento, California

OUTREACH IN PUBLIC LIBRARIES HAS TRADItionally been the purview of only a few staff members. But as libraries become more focused on building community partnerships and collaborations, the need to develop more staff with outreach skills is becoming increasingly important.

Training budgets are limited and must be stretched to meet many competing needs. I conduct many workshops to teach staff about outreach attitudes, skills, and abilities and to lay the foundation for future training. These staff will then train others in their agencies. Sometimes additional training doesn't happen or doesn't happen regularly. Here are some guidelines I've created to help library administrators develop outreach skills in their staff:

1. Training staff to reach out to the community requires both a specific training program and a philosophical commitment. As with any learning process, skills evolve over time.

2. The philosophical commitment begins with prioritizing outreach goals and objectives in the library's strategic plan.

3. The library's operating principles must reflect its outreach objectives. That means its services are planned and evaluated with partners in the com-

munity, outreach to the community is part of everyone's job description, and outreach skills and abilities are a measure of staff performance.

4. Staff members will have diverse levels of awareness, knowledge, and skills in developing outreach competence. Time and support need to be allocated for ongoing self-assessment as a critical part of the outreach training plan.

A formal outreach training program should be highly visible and consistent. A half-day session every six months or a one-day session annually for three to five years is ideal. Each session should cover one or more of the following areas:

> Techniques for engaging the community. Staff should learn how to work with community members as full partners as they determine how to identify and meet the needs of the community.
>
> Techniques for effective communication with a diverse customer base including
>
> - cultural awareness and sensitivity to help develop an understanding of various ethnic and cultural groups and of cultural differences and similarities among them
> - cultural knowledge to help library staff become familiar with selected cultural characteristics, history, values, belief systems, and behaviors of the members of other ethnic or cultural groups (e.g., Latinos, Asians, or people with disabilities)
> - linguistic competence to help staff convey information in a manner that is easily understood by diverse audiences including persons of limited English proficiency, those who have low literacy skills or are not literate, and individuals with disabilities
>
> Techniques for analyzing the library from the community's perspective.

Everything and anything the library does communicates a message to the community. Staff should learn to examine the library's policies, procedures, services, and physical facilities to identify and eliminate barriers to using library services.

Finally, a formal support system must be in place to help staff make full use of the training. Develop a process that creates time and opportunities for staff to practice their outreach skills. Provide opportunities for them to network, mentor, and learn from each other's experiences.

Some people have the interest, confidence, or ability to make outreach a natural part of their jobs. An administrative commitment and a consistent, well-designed training program can help all staff increase their capacity to reach out to the community.

Qualitative Measures of Outreach Effectiveness

Denice Adkins
School of Information Science and
Learning Technologies
University of Missouri, Columbia

THERE ARE SEVERAL QUANTITATIVE WAYS TO measure outreach. You could count all the outreach visits made, the deposit collections placed, or the committee meetings attended. Alternately, you could measure outreach based on the number of people reached: 20 at this class visit, 15 at the story hour at the shelter, 30 who visited the library booth at the street fair last week. Quantitative measures are valuable. They describe what the library has done and how many people the library has reached. Ultimately, however, numbers are an imperfect signifier of library service because they cannot fully represent the relationship between the library and its patrons. To develop a better indicator of that relationship, I will describe a study that I will conduct in the state of Missouri. This study will provide a qualitative measure of outreach services by asking librarians, community gatekeepers, and the target community to describe the outreach experience in their own words and from their own perspectives.

The Latino population, while still a small proportion of the total Missouri population, doubled in size between 1990 and 2000. Many of these new residents have immigrated to Missouri from Mexico to work in the food preparation industry. Missouri librarians do conduct outreach to these new residents, but do not always have a formal assessment system in place to measure the effectiveness of outreach services. The measurement process I propose will involve assessing outreach services at multiple public libraries across the state. Staff at those facilities will be interviewed about the kinds of outreach services they are providing to the Latino population. This first step creates the framework: it documents the services librarians believe they are providing to their patrons and their perceptions of outreach impact.

The second phase identifies gatekeepers within the Latino community—known and trusted figures. Interviews will be conducted with these gatekeepers, who will discuss library services from their points of view. They will be asked how effective the library outreach program has been, whether it meets a real need in the community, and how the library can better serve the Latino population. This phase will document the perceived relevance of library outreach to the community.

Gatekeepers will also be instrumental in setting up the third phase of research: focus groups with Latinos. The gatekeepers will identify people who have participated in some sort of library outreach effort. The focus group will be relatively unstructured, and participants will be encouraged to talk about the library in general, how effective its services are, and what it could do to attract users like them. Library outreach will not be specifically discussed, but if it has been particularly effective, it will probably be mentioned spontaneously. The objective of these focus groups is to give the target outreach audience a chance to discuss their own needs in their own words.

Transcripts and recordings from the interviews and focus groups will be analyzed to demonstrate the specific effects of outreach on the lives of Missouri Latinos. The goal of this project is to demonstrate that outreach makes a difference in the lives of Missouri's Latino population by seeking user testimony that shows a direct link between library outreach programs and benefits to the patrons' lives. More generally, these results will also indicate how outreach can impact the community as a whole. This method of assessment can be replicated by any library, for any population. The results from multiple libraries will provide the proof administrators need to say that outreach services are a success.

Hiring for Outreach

Faye C. Roberts
Columbia County Public Library
Lake City, Florida

How can we find effective staff for library outreach services? Constrained by the dictates of organizational or civil service practices, librarians may need different strategies to hire staff that is committed to the library's mission.

My own views are tempered by my experience as a social worker and a literacy coordinator prior to graduate study in librarianship. I now work in a rural county library that has supported outreach partnerships with the county jail, child care centers, and other community organizations for about two decades. While rural libraries may be a microcosm of issues affecting other libraries, a limited labor pool often compounds their staffing challenges. But there is also an advantage to this limited pool in the opportunity for closer ties to the community, its needs, and its resources.

An illustration of this advantage can be seen in our adult literacy program. In the past decade we've had seven literacy coordinators. Two of them had a master's degree in library information science (MLIS), two others had a four-year degree in education, two had some college, and one had a general equivalency diploma (GED). Both MLIS coordinators supported the outreach concept, but neither was particularly effective in recruiting students or tutors.

In fact, the two coordinators with the least formal education were among the most effective in recruiting and encouraging adult learners—the outreach part of the job. Both related well to nontraditional library users and were sensitive to their problems. One had worked in health and social services. The one with the GED had risen above a troubled youth of her own to have a successful career before returning to school.

To find effective staff we must be creative in (1) developing job descriptions, (2) advertising strategies, (3) selection criteria, and (4) interviewing techniques.

1. A carefully developed job description is key to identifying and evaluating essential skills. Look at job descriptions from social service agencies for new ideas. List all primary tasks, such as "plans and presents programs at various locations" or "delivers materials using library van," along with relevant qualities such as "ability to communicate with people from varied socioeconomic groups" or "knowledge of community agencies."

2. Some qualified people may never hear about library jobs. Consider community partners as referral sources, and remember the effectiveness of word of mouth. In the case of our literacy program, members of the community-based literacy council have been successful recruiters.

3. Look beyond the MLIS degree to find individuals with the skills needed for the job. Better indicators may be previous work in other fields as well as life experience. Those who have worked in social services may have training in listening and counseling beyond the basics of the reference interview. Positive attitude, flexibility, dependability, and the ability to communicate with diverse people may be difficult to codify into a job description but can be spotted during a well-planned interview.

4. The interview should be conducted by a committee, with members who understand how outreach services benefit the target clientele and the special abilities needed to achieve the desired outcome. Find committee members with relevant backgrounds. Choose a parent to interview for a children's librarian, someone who values customer service for a public service opening, or someone from a partnering agency for staff who will work in that partnership. In the interview, ask about experiences that illustrate the applicant's interpersonal skills. Encourage each interviewer to observe both words and body language that indicate attitudes and feelings.

To make our outreach programs more effective, we must change our practices. Changes are generally better tolerated and easier to sustain if they come in small steps. We can address one project or position at a time while keeping an eye on the greater goal of reaching our community.

Training Staff for Job Service Outreach

Bernice Kao
Fresno County Library
Fresno, California

I FIRST JOINED THE FRESNO COUNTY LIBRARY in 2002 after being the career service librarian at Rolling Meadows Public Library in Illinois for 17 years. My assignment was to complete three tasks to make the library's brand-new career center effective in providing much-needed job information for our community.

1. Create dedicated space for a separate career collection, including all current job and career materials and test guides for civil, educational, and professional examinations.
2. Offer job search classes that will cover basic job search, resume writing, and interview skills.
3. Network with government agencies, community organizations, and local businesses to promote awareness and use of the library's employment resources.

Within four months, I had a space next to the reader's services area—a high-traffic location. After another three months I was conducting job search classes.

I developed surveys about employment needs and bookmarks with pathfinders to popular titles and websites. I participated in career days, job fairs, and community job creation projects to publicize the career services at the library. In November 2003, the career center won the California Education and Community Career Center Award for Excellence.

How could the library provide these award-winning services to all patrons in the 32 branches of the county library? And some of the branches, especially in the rural towns, suffer a higher unemployment rate than downtown Fresno. I could not go to every branch to teach the three on-line job search classes. The only way to ensure access to career services at those branches was to incorporate the job search training into a library's staff development program.

I developed a curriculum on principles and practices for finding a job that is divided into four sections: career assessment, research on industry or company, resume writing, and job interviews. Participants find and evaluate career information on the Internet as a supplement to lectures. The class ends with each student doing two job/career assessment exercises in the computer lab. I encourage participants to think about how to connect with agencies in their service areas while working through all four sections. In branches farther outside the city, it's important for staff to mingle with local organizations and to be aware of each community's unique strength and weakness.

I have trained 75 library employees since April 2003, and I plan to continue. This staff development program emphasizes services to everyone, leaving no one behind. Training trainers for job service outreach is a win-win idea for libraries, library staff, patrons, and the business community.

- Training the trainer expands access to job information for residents in rural towns. Branch staff can add their unique community needs into their teaching of job search classes.

- Staff people benefit by learning a new skill. When opportunities for transfer or promotion arise, they will have a winning edge over those who have not been trained to do job service outreach.

- The library as a whole becomes a learning organization. This can become a model for self-improvement, skill-building, and real-life learning.

- The Fresno County business community will enjoy a workforce that is trained to research career opportunities, produce effective resumes, win the interview game, and get hired.

Sharing Skills: Outreach @the Arizona Library Development Division

Jan Elliott
Library Development Division
Arizona State Library, Archives and
Public Records
Phoenix, Arizona

LIBRARY DEVELOPMENT DIVISIONS (LDDs) within state library agencies across the country embody the ultimate in outreach work. In order to be effective, LDD staff must acquire and practice outreach skills in their own work at the state level to support staff at local libraries to do the same. We must practice what we preach.

Library development division consultants at the Arizona State Library, Archives and Public Records (1) model outreach skills in their daily work, (2) promote outreach skills through training, (3) support outreach through grants and statewide programs, and (4) foster outreach by participating in community building events.

Modeling outreach skills to other librarians is a major responsibility for Arizona's LDD staff, who provide advice and professional expertise to libraries via telephone or by site visits. To make each interaction a successful outreach event, the LDD consultant must combine public service skills with professional consultation techniques. This means being approachable, inviting dialog, interviewing to identify issues to be addressed and the results the client desires, and then connecting the client with appropriate resources or people.

LDD personnel *promote* outreach skills by organizing training for library personnel. They seek out exemplary outreach activities practiced within the state or nation and bring those models to the attention of other libraries. Most often this is accomplished in a workshop setting, bringing together project developers and interested librarians who learn what it takes to develop a similar project at their libraries.

The Arizona LDD *supports* local library outreach activities through financial incentives. Competitive grants are awarded to libraries to support the development of programs that offer unique approaches to library outreach. LDD publicizes successful model projects and encourages their adoption by others.

Most LDDs in the United States are known for supporting large-scale outreach activities such as summer reading programs. They create an infrastructure that allows libraries to implement the project with ease by developing program manuals and publicity materials and, in some cases, by providing collection materials.

Eleven years ago, the Arizona LDD established regional economic development information centers in 27 public and community college libraries throughout the state. LDD provided the infrastructure for this project: a well-rounded collection of business reference materials, quarterly training events for the information center librarians, and publicity materials. Collections were continually updated with state and local funding, and electronic databases were added via state library purchases.

This initiative enabled libraries to play a stronger role in the economic development of their region. Economic development information centers are now the venue for monthly business workshops, small business advisories, and research for local entrepreneurs.

Finally, LDDs *foster* outreach by participating in community-building events. In Arizona, this kind of event is epitomized by the Arizona Convocation, an annual event that brings together an ever-widening circle of librarians, museum and historical society directors and staff, tribal archivists, genealogists, library education professionals, students, and interested citizens with the staff of the state library. The two-day event features speakers whose topics reach across professional boundaries and incite discussion. Breakout sessions and unstructured networking time allow individuals to delve deeper into shared issues, develop new allies, and plan projects together.

The convocation is an effective means of outreach for the state library. It allows LDD staff to connect to our colleagues from cultural institutions. All of us benefit from strengthening alliances, building a learning community, creating peer relationships, and sharing resources.

The outreach work of library development staff can best be summed up as "the multiplier effect," an expression coined by Jane Kolbe, director of Arizona's LDD, wherein a small number of library development division personnel devoted to modeling and promoting outreach can make a great impact on the library community. The librarians, in turn, make an even larger impact on the citizens of their state.

Learning by Doing: Outreach Training in a Branch Library

Linda S. Greene
Hiram Kelly Branch
Chicago Public Library
Chicago, Illinois

BUILDING STRONG COMMUNITY LINKAGES IS A priority at the Chicago Public Library. Historically, branch libraries have served as information clearinghouses and forums for important community discussions in their respective neighborhoods. Branches, however, are recognized as partners only if other community organizations and residents know that they exist and what they have to offer. Such recognition is accomplished through community outreach.

At the Hiram Kelly Branch Library, new staff members are introduced to our outreach practices immediately. An overview of the library, the community, and our partnerships are emphasized during orientation. A brief history of the library and the community it serves is always an interesting place to start the discussion about outreach. We always address these questions:

What is the library's role in the community?

How does the community use the library?

How does the community affect library service?

Next, we introduce the branch community partnerships. The library works closely with many agencies, including schools, hospitals, housing and community development corporations, family support agencies, literacy coalitions, block clubs, the park district, and the police department. We use old photos, programs, and fliers to describe past partnerships and collaborations. New staff members learn that coworkers have marched in parades, told stories at mosques, taught computer skills at senior citizen homes, or sponsored literacy nights with a local church. The message we want staff to understand and communicate is that the library, as the cultural backbone of the community, has many free resources and services to help residents.

Then it's time for staff to get their feet wet in the community outreach arena. They attend meetings of community partners. They accompany another employee to a community fair, class visit, or school assembly. The goal of these activities is to make the staff member comfortable with the process of community outreach.

No matter what the event, we make sure that staff understand what we're trying to accomplish by taking part. Whether we're inviting the alderman to an upcoming program, promoting our newsletter, or encouraging parents to bring young children to the library, we let staff know the purpose and desired result of our outreach. On parade day, for example, we try to convey a simple message to the excited crowd: "You can have fun at the library!" "This is where we are!" "Come and see us!" When partnerships develop, staff can see the outcome of the library's outreach for themselves.

It may be obvious that the library and the community benefit from our outreach efforts, but it may not be as clear how staff will benefit from doing outreach. Here, it's a good idea to have other staff members speak of their experiences. A once-shy clerk has become a confident branch representative. Our library paraprofessional speaks about library services at community Youth Net meetings. These skills—creativity, customer service, and public speaking—are useful in the library and any other job arenas. They look good on the resume. As staff members get an idea of how the process works, why we do it, and how everyone benefits, they are encouraged to be outreach ambassadors for the library whenever possible.

Having a community outreach practice and philosophy in the branch library not only establishes partnerships but also creates an inclusive atmosphere in the workplace, adds variety to work duties, and builds skills in a creative way. The library's goal of creating and nurturing community linkages can be fully achieved when community outreach is *everyone's* job.

The Diversity Initiative:
One Committee's Story

Jeanne DeLaney, Judith Cramer,
and Carolyn Evans
Cuyahoga County Public Library
Parma, Ohio

CUYAHOGA COUNTY PUBLIC LIBRARY SERVES 47 suburban Cleveland, Ohio, communities of about 631,000 people through 29 locations. In 1997, a diversity initiatives committee was formed and given this mission:

- identify primary diversity issues facing staff and organization
- recommend initiatives to administration to ensure diversity is reflected in all aspects of the library's operation
- communicate with and support our workforce in implementing diversity initiatives
- serve as diversity program advocates and models of effective behavior

Via application, 16 committee members were selected who represented different races, genders, job levels, and other aspects of diversity. After two years, committee makeup changed: some left, others joined.

The committee met regularly to get to know one another and to establish trust. Guest speakers, including an administrator from a neighboring library system and a library trustee, shared their experiences in implementing diversity initiatives in their work situations. Deborah Plummer and Darryl Tukufu, well-known diversity trainers, were hired as consultants to guide the committee's efforts. A sourcebook, *A Practical Guide to Working with Diversity,* was given to each member.[1] Committee members were sometimes frustrated over the time it took for the group to become focused. We discovered how diverse we were in approaching the subject!

The committee's work also included viewing videos, participating in diversity exercises, and going on field trips. At meetings, members shared holiday traditions, ethnic foods, and personal experiences. After a basic level of trust was established, many shared painful situations they had experienced because of some aspect of their diversity. This broadened our perspective.

In 2000, committee members began to address staff meetings about the work of the diversity initiatives committee. Staff was invited to focus groups led by Darryl Tukufu to identify areas of concern related to diversity. Groups were divided by such areas as race, job positions, gender, and sexual orientation.

Information gleaned from these focus groups, along with industry best practices, became the foundation for daylong workshops coordinated by the committee. The workshops, entitled MOSAIC (Making Our System an All-Inclusive Community), were designed to:

- develop an awareness of our own cultural identity
- enhance our ability to successfully participate and work with differences/similarities and understand how these affect work life
- understand and honor differences/similarities among us and recognize them within ourselves

Workshop agendas included an introduction by the library's executive director, commercially made videos, quizzes, real-life scenarios, and a forum for discussing diversity issues candidly and confidentially.

Nearly 700 staff attended 30 workshops in 2002–3. Immediate evaluations were mixed. Some thought they already had a basic knowledge of diversity and were applying it in work situations. But in surveys taken several months later, many indicated they now thought more frequently of diversity in all aspects of their lives.

Here is a summary of key points and recommendations from the committee's experience:

- Diversity work is a process, not a product.

- Plan for it to take longer than you think.
- The committee should include those with a personal commitment to diversity.
- Periodically include new members to infuse fresh ideas.
- Get buy-in from entire organization (trustees, administration, union leaders, staff) from the beginning.
- Involve staff by gathering data through surveys and focus groups.
- Use an outside consultant, if possible, to bring focus and objectivity.
- Educate committee members about diversity; include activities to facilitate personal disclosure.
- Prioritize goals, objectives, action steps.

NOTE

1. Joy Leach with Bette George et al., *A Practical Guide to Working with Diversity: The Process, the Tools, the Resources* (New York: AMACOM, 1995).

Outreach as Friendship in a Peer-Based Community

Pat Wagner
Pattern Research
Denver, Colorado

To embrace outreach we must start by improving the interactions of staff at all levels inside the library—from part-time shelvers to the director and trustees. We greet everyone, introduce ourselves to each other, and give time for people who are slow to speak. Our goals are to create relationships among peers that demonstrate respect toward all and enable participatory and collaborative decision-making processes.

All outreach training builds on the success of these interactions. Everyone knows how to build peer or equality-based relationships: it is called friendship. Warm smiles, shared interests, breaking bread, celebration, music, dance, art, laughter, time and attention, affection, shared work and problem-solving, asking and giving advice, dialogues on touchy subjects where everyone teaches and learns—most people know how to do these things. They just need encouragement.

Staff also needs to be sensitive to issues of status. Some believe that professional credentials or experience confer privileges of mind and heart over others. It can be subtle, like not asking support staff which books they want, because they don't have a degree in library science. The "professional" library worker might invite support staff members to serve on a joint outreach committee but never to run the committee or make important decisions.

Finally, outreach is not just for the outreach staff. Anyone and everyone can leave the library and seek people on their own turf: listen to their concerns, collect stories, find mentors and champions, and, most important, build friendships.

Friendship in workplaces, inside or outside the library, can respect emotional boundaries as well as the realities of supervisor-employee relationships. We must consider our colleagues as more than just cold professionals or everyone's best friends. Friendship in this context is just a name for peer or equality-based relationships. This means "I see, hear, and understand you to be my equal as a human being."

If our behavior in the workplace and in the community is not based on such friendships, outreach can feel like a token exercise in political and economic expediency. It may seem hypocritical and is likely to breed cynicism among the recipients. It may be revealed by silly mistakes, such as forgetting to ask people their opinions about the quality of the library's services to them.

When all of us—every librarian and library worker—behave as if the people who we are reaching out to are our teachers and partners, we will be able to discard "outreach" programs and rely on a communitywide vision of friendship, built with one human relationship at a time.

SELECTED READINGS

FOLLOWING ARE BOOKS, ARTICLES, AND WEBSITES RECOMMENDED BY CONTRIBUTORS OF *From Outreach to Equity.* More suggested readings can be found at the website of the American Library Association's Office for Literacy and Outreach Services (www.ala.org/olos).

GENERAL

Alire, Camila, and Orlando Archibeque. *Serving Latino Communities: A How-to-Do-It Manual for Librarians.* How-to-Do-It Manuals for Libraries 80. New York: Neal-Schuman, 1998.

de la Penã McCook, Kathleen. "Rocks in the Whirlpool: Equity of Access at the American Library Association." Paper presented to executive board at ALA's 2002 Annual Conference. Available at www.ala.org/ala/ourassociation/governingdocs/keyactionareas/equityaction/rocks whirlpool.htm. Accessed 2 February 2004.

———. "Serving the Demands of Democracy." *Threshold: Exploring the Future of Education* (Winter 2004). Accessed 2 February 2004. www.ciconline.com/AboutCIC/Publications/threshold.htm.

In Plain Language (video). Produced by Dr. Rima Rudd and Dr. William DeJong, Health Literacy Studies Program, Harvard School of Public Health, 2003.

Developed for health care professionals who want to learn about adult literacy and its implications for medicine and public health. It is a good tool for initiating discussion on communication issues. Ordering information at www.hsph.harvard.edu/healthliteracy/video.html.

National Institute for Literacy. "The State of Literacy in America: Synthetic Estimates of Adult Literacy Proficiency at the Local, State, and National Levels." (Last modified 2002.) Available at www.nifl.gov/reders/!intro.htm. Accessed 2 February 2004.

Oregon Library Association, Outreach Round Table. *Outreach Services Handbook 2000.* Rev. ed. Salem, Ore.: The Association, 2000.

Schement, Jorge-Reina. "Imagining Fairness: Equality and Equity of Access in Search of Democracy." In *Libraries and Democracy,* edited by Nancy Kranich. Chicago: American Library Association, 2001.

University of Texas at Austin, School of Information. "Discover Equity of Access." Historical and contemporary information about equity of access issues and efforts in library and information science. Available at www.ischool.utexas.edu/~access. Accessed 2 February 2004.

SERVICES OUTSIDE LIBRARY WALLS

Drumm, John E. "On the Road Again: Presenting the Cybermobile to the World." *Computers in Libraries* 20, no. 1 (2000): 30–32.

Geary, Mike. "Trends in Prison Library Service." *Bookmobile and Outreach Services* 6, no. 1 (2003): 79–91.

Gemmer, Theresa. "Homebound Services: Old Ways and New Ways." *Bookmobile and Outreach Services* 6, no. 2 (2003): 35–40.

Marjamaa, Mary Anne C. "Bookmobile Services to Children and Schools." *Bookmobile and Outreach Services* 4, no. 2 (2001): 7–21.

Martin, Marcella. "Providing Institutional Services." *Bookmobile and Outreach Services* 3, no. 2 (2000): 11–20.

Meadows, Jan. "United States Rural Bookmobile Service in the Year 2000." *Bookmobile and Outreach Services* 4, no. 1 (2001): 47–63.

Pokorny, Renee E. "Library Services to Immigrants and Non-Native Speakers of English: From Our Past to Our Present." *Bookmobile and Outreach Services* 6, no. 2 (2003): 21–34.

Prock, Andy. "Serving the Invisible Population: Library Outreach for Migrant Farm Workers." *Bookmobile and Outreach Services* 6, no. 1 (2003): 37–51.

Tower, Mary L. "Seniors and Mobile Library Services." *Bookmobile and Outreach Services* 3, no. 2 (2000): 37–42.

OUTREACH INSIDE THE LIBRARY

DeCandido, GraceAnne. *Literacy and Libraries: Learning from Case Studies.* Chicago: American Library Association, 2001.

Feinberg, Sandra. *Including Families of Children with Special Needs: A How-to-Do-It Manual for Librarians.* New York: Neal-Schuman, 1999.

Kuharets, Irina A., Brigid A. Cahalan, and Fred J. Gitner, eds. *Bridging Cultures: Ethnic Services in the Libraries of New York State.* Albany, N.Y.: New York Library Association, Ethnic Services Round Table, 2001.

"Policy on Library Services for People with Disabilities." 2001. Written by the Americans with Disabilities Act Assembly, a group administered by the Association of Specialized and Cooperative Library Agencies, a division of the American Library Association. Available at www.ala.org/ala/ ascla/asclaissues/libraryservices.htm. Accessed 2 February 2004.

Selvestone, Harriett. "Equity of Access for All: Serving Our Underserved Populations." *Knowledge Quest* 29, no. 4 (March/April 2001): 5–6.

Stafford, Julie. "The Public Library: Meeting the Personal and Information Needs of Rural Senior Citizens." *Bookmobile and Outreach Services* 6, no. 1 (2003): 19–35.

Walling, Linda Lucas, and Marilyn M. Irwin. *Information Services for People with Developmental Disabilities: The Library Manager's Handbook.* Westport, Conn.: Greenwood, 1995.

Walling, Linda Lucas, and Marilyn H. Karrenbrock. *Disabilities, Children and Libraries: Mainstreaming Services in Public Libraries and School Library Media Centers.* Englewood, Colo.: Libraries Unlimited, 1993.

OUTREACH USING INFORMATION TECHNOLOGY

American Library Association. "Principles for the Networked World." 2003. Available at www.ala.org/Content/NavigationMenu/Our_Association/ Offices/ALA_Washington/Publications16/principles.pdf. Accessed 2 February 2004.

Blackman, Betty J., Stephanie Brasley, et al. "Equity and the Internet: African American Access to the Information Superhighway." *Culture Keepers III: Making Global Connections: Conference Proceedings of the Third National Conference of African American Librarians, July 31–August*

3, 1997 (Newark, N.J.: Black Caucus of the American Library Association), 2000.

Block, Marylaine, ed. *Net Effects: How Librarians Can Manage the Unintended Consequences of the Internet.* Medford, N.J.: Information Today, 2003. Also available at http://marylaine.com/book/index.html. Accessed 2 February 2004.

Calvert, Philip. "Collections for the Information Have-Nots." *Library Collection Development & Management* (September 2003).

The Children's Partnership. "The Search for High-Quality Online Content for Low-Income and Underserved Communities: Evaluating and Producing What's Needed." 2003. Available at www.contentbank.org/research/QualityContent.pdf. Accessed 2 February 2004.

McCloskey, Kathleen M. "Library Outreach: Addressing Utah's 'Digital Divide.'" *Bulletin of the Medical Library Association* 88, no. 4 (Oct. 2000): 367–73. Also available at www.pubmedcentral.nih.gov/articlerender.fcgi?artid=35259. Accessed 2 February 2004.

Nacelewicz, Tess. "Laptops Going Home with Students." *MaineToday.com* Monday, April 8, 2002. Available at news.mainetoday.com/indepth/laptops/020408laptops.shtml. Accessed 2 February 2004.

Roy, Loriene, and David Raitt. "The Impact of IT on Indigenous Peoples." *The Electronic Library* 21, no. 5 (2003): 411–12

Salinas, Romelia. "Addressing the Digital Divide through Collection Development." *Collection Building* 22, no. 3 (2003): 131–36. Also available at http://giorgio.emeraldinsight.com/pdfs/cb223.pdf. Accessed 2 February 2004.

TECHNICAL SERVICES

Berman, Sanford. "Finding Material on 'Those People' (and Their Concerns) in Library Catalogs." *Multicultural Review* (June 2000): 26–28; 48–52. Also available at www.sanfordberman.org/biblinks/gluck.pdf. Accessed 2 February 2004.

Byerley, S. L., and M. B. Chambers. "Accessibility of Web-based Library Databases: The Vendors' Perspectives." *Library Hi Tech* 21, no. 3 (2003): 347–57.

Caplan, Priscilla. *Metadata Fundamentals for All Librarians*. Chicago: American Library Association, 2003.

Greenberg, Jane. "Metadata and the World Wide Web." *Encyclopedia of Library and Information Science*. 2d ed. New York: Marcel Dekker, 2003.

Marcum, Deanna, and Amy Friedlander. "Keepers of the Crumbling Culture: What Digital Preservation Can Learn from Library History." *D-Lib Magazine* 9, no. 5 (2003). Also available at www.dlib.org/dlib/may03/friedlander/05friedlander.html. Accessed 2 February 2004.

Schmetzke, A., guest ed. "Accessibility of Web-Based Information Resources for People with Disabilities." *Library Hi Tech* 20, nos. 2 and 4 (2002).

Slatin, J., and S. Rush. *Maximum Accessibility. Making Your Web Site More Usable for Everyone*. Boston: Addison-Wesley, 2003.

Tenopir, Carol. *Use and Users of Electronic Library Resources: An Overview and Analysis of Recent Research Studies*. Washington, D.C.: Council on Library and Information Resources, 2003. Also available at www.clir.org/pubs/execsum/sum120.html. Accessed 2 February 2004.

Turvey, M. R., and K. M. Letarte. "Cataloging or Knowledge Management: Perspectives of Library Educators on Cataloging Education for Entry-level Academic Librarians." *Cataloging & Classification Quarterly* 34, no. 1/2 (2002):165–87.

ADVOCACY AND OUTREACH

de la Penā McCook, Kathleen. "Reconnecting Library Education and the Mission of Community." *Library Journal* 125, no. 14 (2000):164–65.

———, ed. Community Building, a regular column in *Reference and User Services Quarterly*, published by the American Library Association.

"This column is a forum for sharing examples of public and academic librarians who are actively engaged with community or campus entities to demonstrate how involvement leads to meaningful community-building outcomes."

Kranich, Nancy, ed. *Libraries and Democracy: The Cornerstones of Liberty* Chicago: American Library Association, 2001.

Kretzmann, John P., and John McKnight. *Building Communities from the inside Out: A Path toward Finding and Mobilizing a Community's Assets*. Evanston, Ill.: Asset-Based Community Development Institute, 1993.

Lehman, Kathy. "Promoting Library Advocacy and Information Literacy from an 'Invisible Library.'" *Teacher Librarian* 29, no. 4 (2002): 27–30.

Siess, Judith A. *The Visible Librarian: Asserting Your Value with Marketing and Advocacy.* Chicago: American Library Association, 2003.

www.buildliteracy.org. An interactive website for building and sustaining literacy coalitions, collaborations, and partnerships. BuildLiteracy.org is an initiative of the ALA's Office for Literacy and Outreach Services, with continued support from Verizon.

STAFF DEVELOPMENT

de la Penā McCook, Kathleen. *A Place at the Table: Participating in Community Building.* Chicago: American Library Association, 2000.

Green, Florence J. "Library Outreach Programs in Rural Areas." *Bookmobile and Outreach Services* 5, no. 2 (2002):15–38.

Illinois Literacy Resource Development Center, et al. "The Importance of Assessment for Different Stakeholders." *Adult Literacy Assessment Tool Kit.* Chicago: American Library Association, 2000: 3–4.

Leach, Joy, with Bette George et al. *A Practical Guide to Working with Diversity: The Process, the Tools, and the Resources.* New York: AMACOM, 1995.

Peterson, Lorna. "Using a Homeless Shelter as a Library Education Learning Laboratory: Incorporating Service Learning in a Graduate-Level Information Sources and Services in the Social Sciences Course." *Reference & User Services Quarterly* 42, no. 4 (2003): 307–10.

Sampson, Zora. "The Role of Civility in Diverse Relations." In *Managing Multiculturalism and Diversity in the Library: Principles and Issues for Administrators,* edited by Mark Winston, 93–110. New York: Haworth, 1999.

———. "How Not to Be a Librarian." In *In Our Own Voices: The Changing Face of Librarianship,* edited by Teresa Neely and Khafre Abif, 209. Lanham, Md.: Scarecrow, 1996.

CONTRIBUTORS

Carla D. Hayden, executive director of the Enoch Pratt Free Library in Baltimore, was elected president of the American Library Association for the 2003–4 term. Her presidential initiative focused on equity of access. Hayden chaired ALA's Committee on Accreditation and the Spectrum Initiative to recruit minorities to librarianship. She was named a Woman of the Year by *Ms.* magazine in 2003.

Rhea Brown Lawson is the deputy director of the Detroit Public Library. During her extensive career, she has worked at the Enoch Pratt Free Library and the Brooklyn Public Library and has been a faculty member in the library and information science program at Wayne State University. Lawson received her MLS from the University of Maryland and her Ph.D. in library and information science from the University of Wisconsin.

Jan Meadows, bookmobile supervisor, has worked for the Pikes Peak Library District in Colorado Springs, Colorado, for 17 years. She has been a speaker at bookmobile and outreach conferences and at ALA annual conferences. She was also a facilitator at an ALA preconference in 2002. She is on the editorial board of *Bookmobile and Outreach Services* and writes a bookmobile column on the ALA/OLOS website.

Maureen O'Connor has been involved in outreach services throughout her career and is currently director of programs and services at Queens Borough Public Library. She has worked as a librarian and consultant for the New York State Department of Correctional Services. Before coming to Queens, O'Connor was program officer for literacy and outreach services for the New York State Library.

Satia Marshall Orange is the director of ALA's Office for Literacy and Outreach Services (OLOS). She was the founding director of the Arthur R. Ashe, Jr. Foreign Policy Library at TransAfrica Forum, Washington, D.C., and has been a school and public librarian in Milwaukee, Wisconsin, and Winston-Salem, North Carolina.

Robin Osborne is the outreach services consultant for the Westchester Library System in New York. She facilitates partnerships between public libraries and community agencies and has developed on-line products to provide information to diverse populations, including a Spanish-language website; a bilingual community information directory; and www.firstfind.info, a virtual library of easy-to-read websites.

Kathleen (KG) Ouye is city librarian for the San Mateo Public Library in California. She has worked in four library systems and is the founding chair of the Schools and Libraries Corporation, the body responsible for administering e-rate allocations. Ouye has led many initiatives in developing technology in libraries. She is currently engaged in a $65 million project to build a new main library and renovate branch libraries.

Sandra Rios Balderrama is a recruitment consultant to libraries and the first office manager for Reforma: National Association to Promote Library and Information Services to Latinos and the Spanish-Speaking. She has worked in public libraries for 20 years, in capacities ranging from bookmobile library assistant to coordinator of training and recruitment. From 1998 to 2003, she served as the first director of ALA's Office for Diversity. Rios Balderrama is a storyteller and is learning the art of bird watching.

Zora J. Sampson is the director of library/information and instructional technology at the University of Wisconsin–Barron County in Rice Lake, Wisconsin. She spoke on professional advancement of women and minorities for LAMA at the 1997 ALA Annual Conference and gave a lecture on Civility in Diverse Relations at the Spectrum Leadership Institute in 2002. Sampson has a bachelor's degree in drama and a master's degree in library and information science from the University of Oklahoma.

INDEX